Sophocles
Philoctetes

A new translation and
commentary by Judith Affleck

Introduction to the Greek Theatre
by P.E. Easterling

Series Editors: John Harrison and Judith Affleck

CAMBRIDGE
UNIVERSITY PRESS

CAMBRIDGE UNIVERSITY PRESS
Cambridge, New York, Melbourne, Madrid, Cape Town, Singapore,
São Paulo, Delhi, Dubai, Tokyo

Cambridge University Press
The Edinburgh Building, Cambridge CB2 8RU, UK

www.cambridge.org
Information on this title: www.cambridge.org/9780521644808

First published 2001

A catalogue record for this publication is available from the British Library

ISBN 978-0-521-64480-8 Paperback

PERFORMANCE
For permission to give a public performance of *Philoctetes* please
write to Permissions Department, Cambridge University Press,
The Edinburgh Building, Shaftesbury Road, Cambridge CB2 2RU.

ACKNOWLEDGEMENTS
Thanks are due to the following for permission to reproduce photographs:
p. 14 Musée du Louvre. © Photo RMN, Hervé Lewandowski;
p. 28 Kunsthistorisches Museum, Vienna; p. 39 Paris, Musée d'Orsay.
© Photo RMN, Hervé Lewandowski; p. 80 The National Museum of Denmark;
p. 84 The Metropolitan Museum of Art, Fletcher Fund, 1956. Photo © 1982
The Metropolitan Museum of Art; p. 105 Jean Cocteau Repertory Theater,
New York. Photo © Gerry Goodstein 1997;   p. 115, Fig. A from p. 151 of *The
Cambridge Ancient History, Plates to Volumes V and VI* © Cambridge
University Press. The text on page 104 is reproduced by kind permission of
Faber and Faber Ltd.

Map on p. vii by Helen Humphreys.
Cover picture: *Philoctetes* (1770) by James Barry, courtesy of the Pinacoteca
Nazionale di Bologna.

The author would like to thank Harry Burrett, Tom Jeffery, Alex Jones-Davies,
Will Lawrence, Mike Lesslie, Marcus Littlejohns, Patrick Massey and Charlie
Weston-Simons, the Harrow School cast of *Philoctetes*, October 1999. Also
special thanks to John Harrison, Pat Easterling and Ian McAuslan.

Transferred to digital printing 2009

Contents

Preface

The aim of the series is to enable students to approach Classical
plays with confidence and understanding: to discover the play within
the text.

The translations are new. Many recent versions of Greek tragedy
have been produced by poets and playwrights who do not work from
the original Greek. The translators of this series aim to bring readers,
actors and directors as close as possible to the playwrights' actual
words and intentions: to create translations which are faithful to the
original in content and tone; and which are speakable, with all the
immediacy of modern English.

The notes are designed for students of Classical Civilisation and
Drama, and indeed anyone who is interested in theatre. They address
points which present difficulty to the reader of today: chiefly relating
to the Greeks' religious and moral attitudes, their social and political
life, and mythology.

Our hope is that students should discover the play for themselves.
The conventions of the classical theatre are discussed, but there is no
thought of recommending 'authentic' performances. Different groups
will find different ways of responding to each play. The best way of
bringing alive an ancient play, as any other, is to explore the text
practically, to stimulate thought about ways of staging the plays today.
Stage directions in the text are minimal, and the notes are not
prescriptive; rather, they contain questions and exercises which
explore the dramatic qualities of the text. Bullet points introduce
suggestions for discussion and analysis; open bullet points focus on
more practical exercises.

If the series encourages students to attempt a staged production, so
much the better. But the primary aim is understanding and
enjoyment.

This translation of *Philoctetes* is based on the Greek text, edited by
H. Lloyd-Jones and N.E. Wilson for Oxford University Press. An
asterisk in the translation denotes a missing line; brackets around the
text indicate that these words may have been interpolated. Numbers
in square brackets at the bottom of each page of translation refer to
the lines of the Greek text; line references in the notes and elsewhere
refer to this translation.

John Harrison
Judith Affleck

Background to the story of Philoctetes

(*The names of characters who appear in this play are printed in* **bold**.)

The carvings on the pediments of a fifth century BC temple on the island of Aegina show the legendary wars that took place on the plains of Troy. According to tradition, Troy fell twice: firstly, to an army led by **Heracles**, and secondly, to the 'sons of Atreus', Agamemnon and Menelaus, who commanded a Greek expedition sent to avenge the abduction of Menelaus' wife, Helen, by the Trojan prince, Paris. The heroes of this war were immortalised in Homer's *Iliad*.

Philoctetes belonged to the second generation of besiegers, but was famous in myth for his connection with the first: Heracles, wanting to die to escape the agonising pain of a poisoned robe given him by his wife, Deaneira (the subject of Sophocles' *Trachiniae*), had a funeral pyre built on Mount Oeta. This mountain is in Malis, the home country of Philoctetes and his father, Poeas. Heracles gave his bow and arrows, made famous through his heroic deeds, to Philoctetes in return for lighting this funeral pyre. On his death Heracles was deified.

Other heroes of the second more famous Trojan War were originally reluctant to join the expedition: **Odysseus** feigned madness in an attempt to escape the fighting and Achilles, whose divine mother Thetis knew he was destined to die at Troy, was hidden, disguised as a woman, on Scyros with the daughters of Lycomedes. There he fathered his only child, **Neoptolemus**.

Philoctetes willingly joined the Greek forces with his fleet of seven ships (*Iliad* ii), but before the expedition reached Troy, he was bitten by a snake in the sacred enclosure of the goddess Chryse. His foot became foully infected and his allies abandoned him on the island of Lemnos. This is how Homer tells the story:

Those who lived in Methone and Thaumakia, and held Meliboia and rugged Olizon, these were led by Philoktetes, in seven ships: in each ship fifty rowers had embarked, all skilful fighters with the bow. But Philo-ktetes was lying in an agony of pain on an island, in sacred Lemnos, where the sons of the Achaians had left him suffering from the vile wound of the vicious water-snake's bite. So he lay there in torment: but the Argives in their camp by the ships were soon to remember lord Philoktetes.
(Trans. Hammond)

The action of Sophocles' play takes place not long after the events narrated in the *Iliad* and the subsequent deaths of Achilles and Ajax. These events were told in other epic poems, the *Cypria* and *Little Iliad*, which are now lost. It is the tenth and final year of fighting, the year in which it was prophesied that Troy would fall.

Map of Ancient Greece

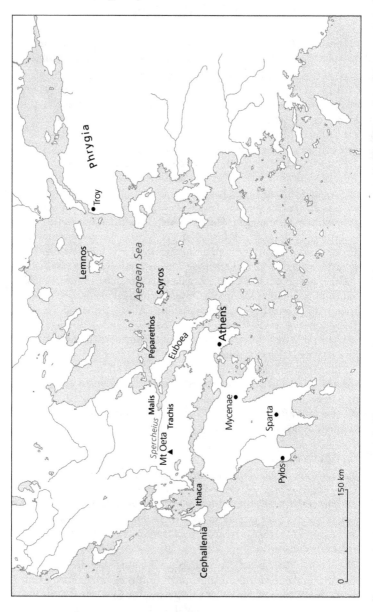

Phrygia

Troy

Lemnos

Aegean Sea

Scyros

Peparethos

Athens

Euboea

Spercheius Malis
Mt Oeta Trachis

Mycenae

Sparta

Itacha

Pylos

Cephallenia

0   150 km

List of characters

ODYSSEUS	*one of the Greek commanders at Troy*
NEOPTOLEMUS	*son of Achilles*
CHORUS	*members of Neoptolemus' crew*
PHILOCTETES	*a Greek commander abandoned on the island of Lemnos by the Greeks*
MERCHANT	*a disguised member of the crew*
HERACLES	*the deified hero*

PROLOGUE (1–138)

The Prologue is the section of the play preceding the entry of the Chorus.

The setting

Most tragedies were set in front of a stage building (*skēnē*), which usually represented a palace or temple, but the opening lines of this play draw attention to the isolation of the setting.

Lemnos was in fact a large, populated island, presented as such earlier in versions of the Philoctetes story by the tragedians Aeschylus and Euripides.

- In lines 1–38 we are given many physical details of the scene. What further impressions do these give?
- How might a sense of isolation be created in a production? Consider in particular the stage set and sound effects.

Fathers and sons

Odysseus' first words to Neoptolemus refer to his famous father, Achilles, recently dead. Odysseus also refers to Philoctetes by his father, **Poeas' son** (5), as well as by his homeland, **Malis** (5). Patronymics, common in epic poetry, are used frequently in this play (see 48, 82, 336, 410). The relationship between fathers and sons will also prove important (see index).

4 I was ordered to do so Odysseus acknowledges to Neoptolemus the part he played in abandoning Philoctetes, but he does not take ultimate responsibility: he claims that this lies with **those in command**: Agamemnon and Menelaus, leaders of the expedition to Troy, also known as 'the sons of Atreus'. (See notes on 383–4 and Responsibility, page 82.)

8–9 offending the gods The enforced exile of Philoctetes is justified by the religious argument that a reverential silence should be kept during sacrifice (see 1068–9).

Dramatic tension

10–11 This is no time for a long story The scene is tense: Odysseus doesn't know where Philoctetes is and cannot afford to risk being seen by him after the part he played in abandoning him. Before briefing Neoptolemus fully he wants to be sure of Philoctetes' whereabouts.

A sense of anticipation is created by Odysseus' references to his plan (12, 21). Neoptolemus – and the audience – must wait for details.

- What impression do you form of the relationship between Neoptolemus and Odysseus from this opening exchange?

12 clever plan Odysseus was traditionally associated in myth with cunning (see Cleverness, page 6); the story of how he tricked the one-eyed Cyclops in *Odyssey ix* is a good example of his quick wit.

ODYSSEUS Here it is – the shore of Lemnos, surrounded by
sea. No one comes here: it's uninhabited. This is where I
left him, Neoptolemus, when your father Achilles was
champion of Greece. I was ordered to do so by those in
command. Poeas' son, from Malis. His foot was oozing pus   5
– some disease was eating through him. We couldn't begin
to make offerings or sacrifice in peace. He kept filling the
whole camp with his wild shouts and screams, offending
the gods.

But why tell you all of this? This is no time for a long   10
story. I think I'm about to catch him, but if he finds me
here, my clever plan is wasted.

Your assistance is needed for the next stage: find the cave
somewhere among these rocks. It has two entrances –
two places to sit and catch the sun when it's cold – but in   15
the summer, a breeze blows through its length, making it
possible to sleep. A little below it, on the left, you should
be able to see a freshwater spring – if it's still there. Make
your way silently and signal to me if he is still living in the
same place – or if he has found somewhere else. Then you   20
can listen while I tell you the rest of what I have to say:
we'll share the work between us.

NEOPTOLEMUS Odysseus, sir, no need to go far to do what
you say! I think I can see a cave like the one you described.

ODYSSEUS Is it up there, or further down? I can't tell.   25

NEOPTOLEMUS Here it is – up here. There's no sound or
trace of anyone nearby.

ODYSSEUS Check he's not asleep inside.

NEOPTOLEMUS It looks like a dwelling, but it's empty.

ODYSSEUS Anything inside to suggest it's inhabited?   30

NEOPTOLEMUS Just some leaves that have been flattened as if
someone had made a bed out of it.

36 This little treasure-trove These ironic words highlight the poverty of Philoctetes' existence.

● How complex is Odysseus' attitude, as revealed in lines 1–45, towards the man he abandoned?

Status
Odysseus' claim that he was acting under orders in lines 4–5 suggested a military hierarchy of command.

● Does this help us understand the relationship between Odysseus, Neoptolemus and the look-out in lines 1–51?

○ What would be the advantages and disadvantages of playing this scene in military dress?

47 Now, if you're ready, tell me what's next Neoptolemus prompts Odysseus to speak now they are confident that Philoctetes will not appear without warning.

The plan
55 Achilles' son Neoptolemus – also known as 'Pyrrhus', for his golden hair (see page 108) – was conceived while Achilles was in hiding with the daughters of Lycomedes. **Home** (56) is Scyros, where Lycomedes was king (see Background to the story, page v).

58–9 they used prayers to get you to leave home … capturing Troy The Greek seer, Calchas, prophesied that Troy could not be taken without the help of Achilles' son. Odysseus and Achilles' old tutor, Phoenix, were sent to fetch him. His name, 'Neo-ptolemus' ('New-to-the-war'), reflects the story that he was a young recruit. Neoptolemus later speaks of his eagerness to go (353–4), hardly surprising given the importance of the Trojan war and the glamour surrounding heroes who fought there.

60 they didn't think you worthy Such a disappointment, in contrast with his high hopes on setting out, perhaps suggests the reality of Neoptolemus' status as an (as yet) unproven hero.

61–2 they gave it to Odysseus After Achilles' death, the Greeks awarded his famous armour to Odysseus (see page 24). Ajax was furious, believing that he had a stronger claim. In revenge, he tried to slaughter the Greek commanders but Athene sent him mad and directed him against the army's livestock instead. His subsequent shame and suicide is the subject of Sophocles' *Ajax*.

64 That won't hurt me! Is this a significant understatement?

66–7 unless we take this man's bow … plain of Dardanus This is the first mention in the play of the famous bow of Heracles (see Background to the story, page v) and of its significance in this play. Dardanus (67) was a son of Zeus and ancestor of the kings of Troy.

● Why does Odysseus say **you** in the second part of this sentence?

ODYSSEUS And otherwise is it empty? Nothing else in there?

NEOPTOLEMUS There is a cup carved from a bit of wood – poor
    work! And some things for lighting a fire.   35

ODYSSEUS This little treasure-trove must be his.

NEOPTOLEMUS Yes, look! Here is something else, drying in
    the sun. Some rags caked in a kind of discharge. Ugh!

ODYSSEUS This is clearly where our man has been living –
    and my guess is he's not far off. How could someone   40
    crippled with an old wound like that get far? He may have
    gone out looking for food, or for some plant he knows of that
    eases his pain.

    Send this man to keep a lookout so that he doesn't catch
    me by surprise. There's no Greek he'd rather find than me.   45

NEOPTOLEMUS He is on his way and will watch out for any
    sign of the man. Now, if you're ready, tell me what's next.

ODYSSEUS Son of Achilles, you are going to have to show
    your quality on this mission – and not only what you're
    made of physically. You may have to help by doing things   50
    that feel strange or unfamiliar. But you're here to assist.

NEOPTOLEMUS What are you asking me to do?

ODYSSEUS You must deceive Philoctetes when you speak to
    him. When he asks you who you are and where you come
    from, tell him you are Achilles' son – there is no need to   55
    disguise that. But say that you are sailing home, that you've
    grown to hate the Greeks and have left their expedition in
    disgust: they used prayers to get you to leave home – you
    were their only means of capturing Troy – but when you
    came, they didn't think you worthy of Achilles' armour,   60
    though you had every right to claim it; they gave it to
    Odysseus. You can say anything you like about me – scour
    your vocabulary for the worst insults you can think of.
    That won't hurt me!

    If you don't do this, you will inflict suffering on all   65
    Greeks: for unless we take this man's bow, you will never
    lay waste the plain of Dardanus. Understand this: *you* can
    win his trust and confidence. I cannot. When you sailed to

69 you were not acting under oath Odysseus, like many who fought at Troy, had been a suitor of Helen. At his suggestion, Helen's father Tyndareus bound all the suitors under oath to defend her should the need arise. Helen married Menelaus, but was later abducted by Paris, son of King Priam of Troy. Odysseus was unable to escape his oath (see Background to the story, page v and note on 1058–9).

Cleverness

The Greek word Odysseus used of his plan in line 12 was *sophisma*; he uses a similar phrase in line 74. Both are related to the word *sophos* (clever), appropriate to Odysseus' traditional attribute: cunning.

However, in fifth-century Athens *sophos* had acquired some negative overtones: the Sophists (teachers of rhetoric, success in public life, etc.) were commonly perceived as misrepresenting truth (e.g. making black seem white) by their clever use of words. In particular, they were satirised and attacked for being morally subversive.

- What is clever about Odysseus' plan?
- In what ways might Odysseus' words in lines 48–81 be considered morally subversive?

89–90 I would rather behave with honour and fail than win a coward's victory More literally, Neoptolemus says that he would rather behave well (*kalōs*) than badly (*kakōs*).

- What do you think Neoptolemus understands by 'well' and 'badly'?

91–2 When I was young Odysseus speaks with the authority of age and experience which can be characterised in many different ways.

○ Try delivering these lines in ways appropriate to: a military commander, a father, a teacher, a politician, a friend. Which seems more appropriate here?
- Consider how in contrast the youthfulness and naïvety of Neoptolemus is revealed in this speech.

Action and talk

93–4 it is always what people say rather than what they do Odysseus meets Neoptolemus' suggestion of using force by drawing a distinction based on the effectiveness of word and action.

The distinction between words and deeds is often made in Homer: a hero should excel both in deed and in his use of words. Odysseus was more renowned for his ability with words, Ajax for his power in action; Achilles excelled in both (see Word and action, page 94).

99–100 And you won't take him by force Odysseus is quick to anticipate further argument in favour of physical action.

- How does Odysseus respond to Neoptolemus' suggestion of persuasion? Why does he seem so sure that Philoctetes is not persuadable?

Troy, you were not acting under oath – you weren't forced
to come, and you were not a part of the original   70
expedition. I am implicated on all these counts. If he sees
me while he has got hold of the bow, I am dead – and so are
you, for being with me.

This is where we have to be clever: how are you going to
steal that invincible bow? I know, boy, it doesn't come   75
naturally to you to be talking like this or to be planning
crimes. But winning it will be sweet – steel yourself. We can
demonstrate our honesty another time. Just for now, for
one little day, forget your principles and follow my lead.
After that you can spend the rest of your life enjoying an   80
unmatched reputation for righteousness.

NEOPTOLEMUS Son of Laertes, I find just listening to this
sort of talk upsetting – and the thought of acting on it is
repellent. I am not, and never have been, the sort to cheat.
And neither, from what people say, was my father. I am   85
ready to use force against the man, but not trickery. With
only one foot he is not going to be able to outmatch all of
us in a fight! I was sent to do this job with you, and I don't
want to be called a traitor, but I would rather behave with
honour and fail than win a coward's victory.   90

ODYSSEUS You are the son of a noble father. When I was
young, I, too, preferred action to talk. These days I see
that when it's put to the test, it is always what people say
rather than what they do that makes the difference.

NEOPTOLEMUS You are asking me to tell lies?   95

ODYSSEUS I am telling you to trick Philoctetes.

NEOPTOLEMUS Why must I trick him? Why can't I use
persuasion?

ODYSSEUS He will never be persuaded. And you won't take
him by force.   100

NEOPTOLEMUS What makes him so confident of his strength?

ODYSSEUS Deadly arrows from which there is no escape.

NEOPTOLEMUS No one dares even go near him?

ODYSSEUS I've told you: your only chance is to trick him.

NEOPTOLEMUS And you don't think it shameful to lie?   105

Means and ends

In eliminating the use of force and persuasion, Odysseus has
simplified his argument: there is only one means of ensuring the
success of the mission – deception. All that remains is for him to
convince Neoptolemus that the fulfilment of the mission is essential.
In contrast to his view of Philoctetes (line 99), he sees Neoptolemus as
persuadable.

- Does what we have seen of Neoptolemus' character so far suggest
  that Odysseus will find him easy to persuade?

125 All right. I'll do it

- How does Odysseus persuade Neoptolemus?

132–3 the same man, but disguised to look like a merchant The
merchant appears later in the play (lines 516–17).

137 Hermes, god of tricks Hermes, the messenger of the gods, was
also associated with travellers, merchants and tricksters.

137–8 Athene Polias … goddess of victory Odysseus' patron goddess
appears frequently in the *Odyssey* (e.g. *Odyssey xiii* 221–440). The
epithet 'Polias' refers to her protection of the *polis* (city-state). She
gave her name to Athens and was celebrated there in particular as
Athēnē Nikē (goddess of victory). In this play, Odysseus has certain
qualities and characteristics seen in Homer's Odysseus, such as
cunning (see Cleverness, page 6 and note on line 12) and the support
of Athene.

Review of the Prologue: characterisation

- When Neoptolemus revolts against the expectation that he should
  lie in lines 82–108, how clearly thought through do his objections
  seem? What age do you think an actor playing the role should be?
- How might an actor playing Neoptolemus respond to Odysseus'
  words in lines 48–126? In particular, how can the shift from line
  107 to 126 be made dramatically convincing?
- Read through or act out the Prologue twice.
  i) Make Odysseus as sinister a character as you can.
  ii) Make him as sympathetic as possible.
  Which 'version' works better?
- Which words do you feel are best suited to the character of
  Odysseus: *sinister, sympathetic, wily, ruthless, charming, pragmatic,
  cowardly, amoral, concerned, bullying, confident*?
- Are there any significant differences in the relationship between
  Neoptolemus and Odysseus at the beginning and end of the
  Prologue?

ODYSSEUS Not if that lie means safety.

NEOPTOLEMUS How can anyone have the face to say such things?

ODYSSEUS When what you are doing is for a profitable end, there's no need to hesitate. 110

NEOPTOLEMUS And what profit am I going to get out of his coming to Troy?

ODYSSEUS His bow is the only thing that will take Troy.

NEOPTOLEMUS So I am not the one – as I was always told – who is going to destroy Troy? 115

ODYSSEUS You can't do it without the bow, but the bow is useless without you.

NEOPTOLEMUS If that is so, then I suppose we must hunt it down.

ODYSSEUS If you succeed in this, you will take home two prizes. 120

NEOPTOLEMUS What are they? Once I know I won't be able to refuse.

ODYSSEUS You will win a reputation for wisdom, as well as bravery.

NEOPTOLEMUS All right. I'll do it. I'll set aside my sense 125
that it's wrong.

ODYSSEUS Now you're sure you remember what I told you?

NEOPTOLEMUS Of course. I've agreed now – once and for all.

ODYSSEUS You stay and wait for him here. I'll go in case I
am seen with you, and I'll take the look-out back to the 130
ship. I will send him back again if you seem to me to be
taking too long – the same man, but disguised to look like a
merchant. The deception may help us. He'll spin some
fanciful tale. You, boy, pick up on anything useful he says
as he goes along. 135
I'm off back to the ship. I am handing over to you.
May Hermes, god of tricks, guide us both. And Athene
Polias, too, goddess of victory, who always takes care of me!

PARODOS (ENTRY OF THE CHORUS) (139–242)

This is the section where the Chorus first appear through the *parodoi* (entrances) and onto the *orchēstra* (circular dance floor) singing to musical accompaniment (see pages 114–16). The Chorus in Greek plays were made up of 12–15 men. They are present throughout the rest of the play, commenting on and punctuating the action through music and dance.

The Chorus in *Philoctetes* consist of members of Neoptolemus' crew, who interact with their young commander throughout this opening lyric (musical) section.

They begin by asking for instructions, tactfully reminding Neoptolemus of his responsibilities (139–50). Neoptolemus offers to show them the cave and tells them to keep alert (151–9). They reassure him that they are ready to do whatever is required and question him further (160–7).

The Chorus in *Philoctetes* sailors or islanders?

An essay by the first century AD Greek orator Dio Chrysostom compares versions of the story of Philoctetes' removal from Lemnos by the three great tragedians of the fifth century BC, Aeschylus, Euripides and Sophocles. Two of the three plays are now lost. Dio draws a number of comparisons which are of particular interest since Sophocles wrote his version last (in 409 BC) and would presumably have been aware of how the story had been handled earlier.

One significant difference is in the composition of the Chorus. Sophocles is alone in making them consist not of islanders from Lemnos, but of sailors who have arrived with Odysseus and Neoptolemus.

- Look at the note on The setting, page 2 and consider why Sophocles decided to make his Chorus consist of sailors from another land.
- When you have read the *parodos* (139–242) consider how this decision affects our view of a) Philoctetes and b) Neoptolemus.

141 The man will be suspicious The Chorus are well informed. This is strange in that they must either have overheard the conversation between Odysseus and Neoptolemus or have been briefed earlier. It would have been highly unconventional for the Chorus to be on stage before the *parodos*.

142–3 What should we say? What should we hide? They also seem aware of the deceptive nature of the mission.

139 sir 148 lad The Chorus address Neoptolemus as their commander and make a direct reference to his god-given authority (145–9), but their reference to him as 'lad' makes it clear that they are older. Some may have served with Achilles.

167 catches us by surprise The Chorus use the same phrase as Odysseus did in lines 44–5, maintaining the atmosphere of suspense.

CHORUS   What's to be done, sir?
          We're strangers here on strange land.   140
             The man will be suspicious:
               What should we say?
              What should we hide?
                 Tell us.

                Men who rule   145
     Have more skill and judgement than others:
    Zeus gives them their god-like authority.
        This power has come to you, lad,
           From time immemorial.
       So tell us how we can serve you.   150

NEOPTOLEMUS   For now, you might like to see
          The place where he sleeps,
             Here by the shore.
        Don't be afraid, have a look.

        When the strange wanderer   155
          Who's left this shelter
             Comes back,
        Come forward on my signal.
        Try to be at hand to help.

CHORUS   What you ask has long been our concern, sir: 160
        To keep an eye on your every need.
             Now, tell us,
      What kind of place does he live in?
           Where is he now?
        It would help us to know   165
       In case he suddenly appears,
      And catches us by surprise.

When the Chorus see the cave they begin to feel pity and, together with Neoptolemus, try to imagine what Philoctetes' existence must be like (168–94). The Chorus see Philoctetes' change of fortune as some divinely ordained retribution (195–8).

170 Are there any tracks …? The play is full of the language of hunting (see also lines 118–19, 167 and index). The Chorus search for Philoctetes and his bow as for a wild animal.

174 A rocky cave he sleeps in The situation resembles that in *Odyssey ix* when Odysseus and his crew discover the cave of the Cyclops and nervously await the arrival of the owner.

175 Two entrances Odysseus made the same point in 14. The double entrance adds suspense to the hunt since Philoctetes could approach his cave from more than one direction. In the original production the *skēnē* may have represented the cave with one mouth facing the *theātron* (viewing area) and the other presumably out of sight (see page 16).

196–8 How the generations of man suffer / When mortal life / Exceeds the bounds of moderation! The Chorus express a general idea, common in tragedy, that excess is dangerous and liable to punishment from the gods. Pentheus in Euripides' *Bacchae* and Ajax in Sophocles' play of the same name are examples of men who fall victim to the gods because they overreach themselves. Mortals do not necessarily have the capacity to appreciate what 'excess' in this sense is; the Chorus make no specific conjecture about what has led to Philoctetes' suffering.

	Where does he go?	
	Where does he rest?	
	Are there any tracks	170
	Inside or out here?	

NEOPTOLEMUS This is his home.
You can see it:
A rocky cave he sleeps in.
Two entrances.   175

CHORUS   Poor fellow!
Where can he have gone?

NEOPTOLEMUS He must be out looking for food,
Dragging that foot,
Furrowing the ground.   180
He may be quite near.
This is how they say he makes his living:
A wretch hunting wretchedly for game
With his winged arrows.
No one comes near   185
To heal his sufferings.

CHORUS   I feel sorry for him.
No one to care for him,
No companion to watch over him.
Miserable and alone always,   190
Sick from his savage infection.
Bewildered as every new need arises,
How does he cope?
How does the poor wretch cope?

This is the work of the gods!   195
How the generations of man suffer
When mortal life
Exceeds the bounds of moderation!

The Chorus dwell in particular upon the cruelty of Philoctetes' enforced lack of human contact (199–207). Neoptolemus attributes the original punishment to a specific goddess, Chryse, and conjectures more generally that the gods must be keeping Philoctetes away from Troy until the time when the city is due to fall. These thoughts are interrupted by cries of pain, which become increasingly distinct.

207 Babbling Echo Echo is frequently personified in myth, most famously in the story of Narcissus. Rejected by Narcissus, who loved only his own reflection, she wasted away with grief until nothing but her voice remained. Her indiscriminate sound offers Philoctetes no human comfort; it merely emphasises the rocky emptiness of the island.

211 Chryse Philoctetes was bitten by a snake on Chryse, a small island (now submerged) which lies between Lemnos and Troy (see map, page vi), while performing a sacrifice to the goddess also known as Chryse (see illustration below).

Cries offstage

The arrival of Philoctetes, anticipated since the opening lines of the play, is heralded by his cries. A similar dramatic effect is used in *Ajax* (333–43) and in Euripides' *Medea* (96–168).

- What dramatic opportunities are there here? Consider how the sailors and Neoptolemus might react to the sound. How might the cries affect our view of a) Philoctetes and b) Neoptolemus' task?

Philoctetes bitten by the snake. Red figures stamnos by Hemonax (c. 450 BC).

He came from a noble family,
Perhaps second to none in his birth. 200
Now he has lost everything in his life
And lives alone, with
Wild deer and shaggy goats for company.
Pitiful in his hunger, in his pain,
With no rest or release from his torments, 205
He cries bitterly, but, far off, only
Babbling Echo responds.

NEOPTOLEMUS None of this seems strange to me.
If I'm right, his sufferings
Were sent by a god, 210
By harsh Chryse.
As for what he feels now,
With no one protecting him,
It must be that one of the gods
Is concerned that he should not aim 215
His divine, invincible arrows at Troy
Until the time is right –
The day when they say the city must fall to his bow.

CHORUS Quiet, lad!
NEOPTOLEMUS What is it? 220
CHORUS A noise.
A familiar sound to one
whose constant companion is pain.

Here? Or was it here?
I hear it! I hear it! 225
A clear sound.
Someone crawling in discomfort
The oppressive cry of a weary man,
Far off, but distinct,
Signalling his pain. 230
Ready, son?

The Chorus are alarmed and uncertain as to how to respond as Philoctetes finally appears on stage.

237 And that's no shepherd in the fields This incongruous picture, like the image of ploughing at 180, serves as a reminder of how 'uncivilised' a being we are about to encounter: his means of survival are wholly primitive. The sailors' ironic comment also emphasises the harshness of Philoctetes' cry in contrast with the harmonious sounds of a pipe.

The appearance of Philoctetes

The first sight of Philoctetes is a moment of dramatic impact, from wherever he appears. If the *skēnē* represented the cave in the original production (see note on 175), then his appearance might have the effect of sudden surprise. An entrance through one of the *parodoi* (side-entrances) would give the audience more time to study the ravaging effects of ten years' isolation.

- How might somebody actually appear under these circumstances in terms of clothing, hair, body, movement, facial features?
- How would you stage this entry? How would the Chorus respond to it? Would Philoctetes speak straight away?

NEOPTOLEMUS	What?
CHORUS	Use your wits!

What do we do now?

He's not far off…   235

Almost here.

And that's no shepherd in the fields playing his pipe!

His cry carries far and wide

As he's made to stumble,

Or scans the bay   240

Which welcomes no ship.

A terrible cry.

FIRST EPISODE PART 1 (243–387)

Episodes are scenes played by the actors. They are divided off from each other by major choral odes (*stasima*).

Philoctetes' first words

Circumstances may have reduced Philoctetes to a primitive level of existence and appearance, but his words are civilised: he recognises their language and clothes, understands the impact his appearance is likely to have on them and uses the language of friendship (249–50).

Silence?

The impact of this speech could vary considerably in production: is it a nervous, unbroken barrage of questions or does Philoctetes give the strangers the chance to reply?

● What difference would punctuating the speech with silences make?

254 What sweeter sound! In Euripides' version of the play, Philoctetes was ready to shoot any Greek who came near him. The delight of Sophocles' hero at hearing Greek is touching.

261–2 the child of my dearest friend ... Old Lycomedes These remarks, full of warmth and friendliness, hardly make Neoptolemus' task easier! As a close friend of Achilles, Philoctetes stands in a similar position to Neoptolemus as Odysseus: both are possible father-figures to whom Neoptolemus might look for guidance and support. Lycomedes was Neoptolemus' maternal grandfather and King of Scyros, where Neoptolemus grew up (see Background to the story, page v).

War orphans

In fifth-century Athens, the children of men killed in war ('war orphans') were educated by the state and at state expense. When these children reached manhood they played a significant part in the dramatic festival, the City Dionysia (see Introduction to the Greek Theatre, page 114), by parading with the new weapons with which the state had provided them. Neoptolemus' age and status make him the heroic equivalent of these young men. This play may have encouraged reflection from the audience about the responsibilities of the state and the education of such youths.

PHILOCTETES Strangers! Who are you? Why has your ship
landed here? There's nowhere safe to anchor. No one lives
here. Who am I talking to? What's your homeland? Your   245
family? Your clothes are Greek. Beloved Greece! But I want
to hear you speak. Don't be afraid or shrink back. Don't be
shocked by my wild appearance. Pity me, instead. I am alone
and wretched: deserted, injured, without a single friend. Speak,
if you have come in friendship. Answer me. I have spoken to   250
you – it is only fair that you should respond.

NEOPTOLEMUS Friend, know first that we *are* Greeks. That is
what you wanted to know.

PHILOCTETES What sweeter sound! Think of it! After all this
time, to be greeted by a fellow Greek! What brought you here,   255
boy? What made you land? Were you blown here? Blessed
wind! Tell me everything – I want to know who you are.

NEOPTOLEMUS My family come from the island of Scyros. I
am sailing home. People know me as the son of Achilles
– Neoptolemus. That's all there is to know.   260

PHILOCTETES Then you are the child of my dearest friend, and
from a land I love. Old Lycomedes must have looked after you!
But what has made you land here? Where have you come from?

The first lie

Neoptolemus' first pretence – that he has not heard of Philoctetes – was not instructed by Odysseus and is not strictly necessary; it causes Philoctetes great pain.

- Why do you think Neoptolemus pretends not to have heard of Philoctetes?

kleos (fame)

When Neoptolemus decided to deceive Philoctetes at lines 125–6 he did so out of consideration for *kleos*: for how he would be known. Philoctetes' *kleos* consists in being **son of Poeas** and **the man who mastered the bow of Heracles** as he reasserts in 279–81. The word is frequently used in Homer when talking about a hero's glorious reputation. In *Iliad ix* Achilles recognises that he faces the hero's choice between a life that is short but which brings undying *kleos*, or a long life without glory (see page 102). In 273–7 Philoctetes imagines a conspiracy of silence: his enemies have deprived him of *kleos*, so that the new young generation will never know the crime they have committed in abandoning a fellow fighter; but the laughter of his enemies seems to hurt him even more.

276 breaking every law of god Philoctetes' statement contrasts strikingly with Odysseus' most powerful justification for abandoning him (see 6–9).

277 my sickness thrives Philoctetes speaks of his disease as of something alive and independent (see also **hungry, feeding** in 320). His speech is often idiosyncratic: the paradox in the idea of the essentially destructive sickness thriving is one example (see note on Language, page 70).

- Does this give an actor any clue as to how he might create a 'voice' for Philoctetes?

282 Lord of Cephallenia He means Odysseus: Cephallenia is an island near Odysseus' home, Ithaca.

285 Chryse The island where Philoctetes was bitten (see note on 211).

292–4 You, boy – can you imagine ... Picture me Philoctetes makes it difficult for Neoptolemus not to become emotionally involved in his tale of misery.

- How might an actor playing Neoptolemus respond to this direct address? What is the difference in dramatic impact of turning to face the speaker or of looking away?

NEOPTOLEMUS Troy. I am heading away from Troy.

PHILOCTETES I don't understand. You didn't sail in our original 265
expedition to Troy.

NEOPTOLEMUS Did you take part in that ordeal?

PHILOCTETES Child, do you not know who you are looking at?

NEOPTOLEMUS How should I know a man I've never set eyes on?

PHILOCTETES Haven't you ever even heard my name? Not 270
heard any word of the misfortunes which ruined me?

NEOPTOLEMUS I'm sorry. I don't know what you mean.

PHILOCTETES More suffering! The gods must truly hate me! So
no news of how things are with me has reached home, or
filtered through to anywhere in Greece? The men who cast 275
me out, breaking every law of god, hold their tongues – and
laugh. Meanwhile my sickness thrives, and gains strength all
the time.

Oh, child! Son of Achilles, you must have heard of *me*! I am
the man who mastered the bow of Heracles – Philoctetes, son 280
of Poeas. The man whom those two generals – along with the
Lord of Cephallenia – shamelessly cast out, destitute, wasting
away from a savage wound, maimed by a murderous snake's
vicious bite.

The fleet had left the island of Chryse and put in here. This is 285
where they abandoned me, alone with my wound. They
went off and were glad when they looked back from the open
waters to see me sleeping on the shore, here, under this arched
rock. Yes, they deposited me and sailed away, throwing me a
few rags fit for an outcast and a little food. I hope they meet 290
with as much luck themselves one day!

You, boy – can you imagine what it was like for me, waking up
here after they'd gone? Getting up that day? Imagine the tears,
the cries of anguish. Picture me, seeing the ships I had
travelled with all gone and not a soul here: no one to help me; 295
no one to ease the weariness of my affliction.

Savagery and civilisation

308–9 ... provide me with everything Philoctetes describes, with a hint of pride, how he has found shelter, food, water and fire. This subsistence level of existence contrasts with the aspects of civilised society (trade and hospitality) he mentions in lines 311–12.

● What other aspects of civilised life are missing on Lemnos?

Aristotle's definition of man

Aristotle, writing in the fourth century BC, famously defined man as a *politikon zōon* : as essentially a part of a social structure, the *polis*. He uses the following analogy to explain his meaning:

> Separate hand or foot from the whole body, and they will no longer be hand or foot except in name, as one might speak of a 'hand' or 'foot' sculpted in stone ... [they] no longer have the capacity and function which define [them].
>
> *Politics* 1253a18 (trans. Sinclair/Saunders)

A man incapable of participating in the *polis* is a mere animal; a 'man' in name only. A man so self-sufficient that he has no need of human society (the *polis*) would be a god.

● What aspects of Philoctetes' nature make him unmistakably a man by Aristotle's definition, despite his isolation?

322 I hope one day the gods Here and in 290–1 Philoctetes curses the Greeks who abandoned him. This is the second reference in this speech to the gods (see note on 276).

● Is this simply a figure of speech or does Philoctetes still seem, despite his fate, to have confidence in the just powers of the gods?

Response to Philoctetes' speech

The Chorus respond first, in tones of pity – an emotion not expressed by Neoptolemus. Cleverly briefed by Odysseus, he picks up instead on Philoctetes' last words (320–2) and launches upon the essential part of his deception: that of establishing a bond of trust with Philoctetes.

○ What would you expect Neoptolemus and the Chorus to be thinking or feeling as they listen to Philoctetes' speech (273–323)? What distinctions might a director make in their respective responses?

329 You've had the same experience? Philoctetes swallows the bait eagerly and, with his subsequent, unsuspecting questions, is generally helpful in giving Neoptolemus the chance to warm to his theme.

Everywhere I looked I found nothing except my own misery.
And of this, child, there was plenty!

So time passed, and I had to get by on my own in this little
cave. The bow provided me with my stomach's needs. I'd   300
shoot birds overhead or anything else I could get with an
arrow, then twist my way towards it, wretchedly, dragging my
foot behind.

And when I needed a drink, or a winter frost struck and I
had to get fire-wood, I'd crawl out and manage somehow.   305
When there was no fire, I'd work hard, striking one stone
against another until I'd made a hidden spark shine out. That
is what has kept me alive: that fire and this dwelling provide
me with everything – except release from my disease.

Now, boy, I'll tell you about the island. Sailors don't come   310
near it if they can help it. There's no anchorage, nowhere for
sailors to trade and nowhere to stay. No one with any sense
makes the journey here. Suppose someone lands without
meaning to – it's bound to happen, quite often, perhaps, in
the span of a man's long life. When they come, child, they   315
say they feel sorry for me. Maybe they even give me a share
of their food or something to wear – out of pity. But when I
mention it, no one will do what I ask, and take me home.
This is the tenth year that I have been dying here, wretched
and hungry, feeding this insatiable wound on my misery. This   320
is what the sons of Atreus and the power of Odysseus have
done to me, child. I hope one day the gods on Olympus make
them suffer as they have made me.

CHORUS   Like those who have come before, I pity you, son of
Poeas.   325

NEOPTOLEMUS   And I can bear witness that what you say is
true. I myself have met with trouble at the hands of Atreus'
sons and the powerful Odysseus.

PHILOCTETES   You've had the same experience? You, too, have
just cause for anger against that destructive pair?   330

332 Mycenae ... Sparta ... Scyros Agamemnon and Menelaus (the sons of Atreus) were kings of Mycenae and Sparta respectively. Scyros is where Neoptolemus was raised. (See map, page vi.)

The death of Achilles

This event is foreshadowed in the *Iliad* but not described there. Paris, the Trojan prince who abducted Helen and precipitated the war, is said to have shot Achilles with an arrow in the heel under the direction of Apollo. Vase paintings show the hero's body rescued from the fighting and carried off the field by Ajax while Odysseus fights off the Trojans. The importance of rescuing a body lay in being able to provide a proper burial (the final two books of the *Iliad* illustrate the importance of this in the Homeric world), but also in preventing the body from being stripped of arms by the enemy. Achilles' weapons were of particular value since they were forged for him by the god Hephaestus at the request of his mother Thetis (*Iliad xviii*). These were awarded to Odysseus after they were rescued (see note on lines 61–2).

342 Apollo God of archery, prophecy and the arts. He supported the Trojans during the Trojan War.

350 the godlike Odysseus and my father's old tutor Godlike is frequently used as an epithet for Odysseus in the *Odyssey* and perhaps genuinely reflects how he first appeared to Neoptolemus, but the tone here is presumably ironic. Achilles' tutor, Phoenix, went with him to Troy. Achilles' feelings of affection and trust for the old man are clear in *Iliad ix* when Phoenix forms another embassy, together with Odysseus and Ajax, trying to persuade Achilles to rejoin the fighting (see page 102, *Kleos* sacrificed).

352–3 the gods would allow no man but me to capture the citadel At what point do you think Neoptolemus' account of how he came to Troy becomes untrue? Can we be sure? (See note on Audience uncertainty: the arms of Achilles, page 26.)

359 Sigeum The promontory near Troy where Achilles was buried.

NEOPTOLEMUS Yes – an anger I'd like to settle with them one
day. Mycenae and Sparta can learn then that Scyros, too, is
the mother of strong men!

PHILOCTETES Well said, boy. What is their crime? What has
provoked this outbreak of passion? 335

NEOPTOLEMUS Son of Poeas, I'll tell you, though it's hard to
find the words. I'll tell you how I went only to be greeted by
insults from them when Achilles met his fate and died.

PHILOCTETES Ah, no. Don't tell me any more until I know
this first: Peleus' son is dead? 340

NEOPTOLEMUS Yes. No man killed him. It was a god. They
tell me he was hit by an arrow, brought down by Apollo.

PHILOCTETES A noble killer for a noble victim. But I don't
know what to do first, child: question you or mourn for him?

NEOPTOLEMUS It seems to me you have troubles enough of 345
your own, without lamenting those of your friends.

PHILOCTETES You are right. Then go back to the beginning
and tell your story again. How did they insult you?

NEOPTOLEMUS They sailed to find me in a finely rigged ship,
the godlike Odysseus and my father's old tutor. They told me 350
– I don't know if it was true or not – that since my father had
died the gods would allow no man but me to capture the
citadel. They were so insistent! And anyway, they could
hardly restrain me from setting out straight away. I wanted,
more than anything, to see his body before it was buried. I had 355
never seen him. And on top of that, there was the glory, if I
should go and be the one to capture the citadel of Troy!
After two days' journey, sailing with a good wind, I put in at
Sigeum, that hateful place. As I disembarked, the whole army
crowded around me and greeted me, swearing that it was 360
Achilles they saw, alive again. But he was dead, and I, unhappy
son, wept for him.

Audience uncertainty: the arms of Achilles (See also notes on lines 61–2 and The death of Achilles, page 24.)

The picture on page 28 shows Odysseus handing over the arms of Achilles to Neoptolemus. This may have happened as soon as Neoptolemus arrived at Troy, but there is nothing in the play to indicate certainly that Neoptolemus is in possession of his father's arms yet. In at least one version of the story he seems not to receive them: Pausanias (I.xxxv.4) tells a story of how Odysseus was shipwrecked and the arms were washed up on Ajax's tomb.

The audience is left feeling uncertain in a number of ways during the course of the play (see also The prophecy, page 98). On this particular occasion we might wonder about the following: *Did* Neoptolemus ask for the arms? *Were* they refused him? Is Neoptolemus a supremely good liar on whom Odysseus knew he could depend, or has Odysseus ensured a convincing performance by playing on areas of genuine sensitivity?

- How many of these questions have to be resolved in performance?
- In some types of drama, e.g. thrillers, detective films, the director deliberately keeps the audience guessing. What is the effect here?

382 vicious man of vile descent! The alliteration of the original Greek is striking: *kakistou kak kakōn* (see note on *kakos*, page 100). Neoptolemus does his best to fulfil the instructions Odysseus gave in 62–3 and includes general abuse about his descent, alluding to the tradition that Odysseus' real father was not Laertes but the infamous Sisyphus (see note on 411).

383–4 An army, like a state, depends on its leaders Neoptolemus' words recall Odysseus' lines at the opening of the play (see lines 4–5).

- Is Neoptolemus directing Philoctetes' hatred away from Odysseus towards Agamemnon? Is he aware of the corrupting power Odysseus has had upon himself? Or does the audience have a fuller understanding of Neoptolemus' words than the speaker himself (dramatic irony)? (See also note on *kakos*, page 100.)

For the original audience there were almost certainly contemporary political overtones: Sophocles' *Philoctetes* was produced in 409 BC, four years after the Athenian defeat in Sicily and in the aftermath of an oligarchic coup in 411 (democracy was restored in 410). Leaders like the arrogant and charismatic Alcibiades were treated with suspicion – and so were their teachers (see note on Cleverness, page 6).

Two tales of suffering

- Apart from the focus on Odysseus and the sons of Atreus, what do the two tales of suffering (273–323 and 349–87) have in common? How are they dissimilar?

After a little while I approached the sons of Atreus,
thinking them my friends. I asked them for my father's
weapons and anything else he had. They said... they spoke   365
without any sense of shame, 'Son of Achilles, you can take
the rest of your father's things, but another man is now
master of his weapons: Laertes' son, Odysseus.' With tears in
my eyes I sprang up to face them, hurt and angry. 'Thieves!
How dare you hand my armour to someone else without   370
consulting me?' Odysseus spoke up. He happened to be there.
'Yes, boy. And they were right to present me with those arms.
I saved them and his body. I was there.' I was furious.
Straight away I tore into him, every curse I knew – leaving
nothing out. Did he really think he could rob me of my   375
armour? He is not a man who angers easily, but at this, stung
by my words, he replied, 'You weren't with us. You were
somewhere else, and should not have been. And after this
insolent talk you'll never sail home to Scyros with this
armour now.' His insults ringing in my ears, I set sail for   380
home. Robbed of what was rightfully mine, a victim of
Odysseus, that vicious man of vile descent! [But I don't hold
him as responsible as those in command. An army, like a
state, depends on its leaders: men are led astray and become
corrupt because of what their teachers tell them.]   385
That's all I have to say. Anyone who hates Atreus' sons is
my friend – and the gods' too, I pray.

FIRST CHORAL INTERLUDE (388–98)

The first episode is punctuated by two short lyric passages sung by the Chorus (see pages 29 and 37). Both passages follow the same metrical pattern, just as passages within the longer *stasima* (see also page 50) are paired metrically as *strophe* and *antistrophe*.

The Chorus invoke the great goddess Earth to witness the appeals they claim to have made when the sons of Atreus refused Neoptolemus the arms of Achilles.

● How do the Chorus' words affect our view of what Neoptolemus has just said?

● Are the Chorus here merely commenting on the action (see note on the usual role of the Chorus, page 10) or are they fully involved in it? How might a director respond to different levels of involvement from the Chorus?

388 Earth, mother of all Earth (also known as Ge, Gaia and Rhea) was mother to the Titans by her own child, Heaven (Uranus). Saturn (Cronus) was the last to be born. As 'Rhea' she then bore to Cronus several of the Olympian gods, including Zeus.

391 Ruler of Pactolus ... mistress of bull-devouring lions Earth is here also identified with Cybele, a fertility goddess associated with Phrygia, the area of Asia Minor which includes Troy and the gold-bearing river Pactolus. She is sometimes represented in a chariot drawn by lions.

Neoptolemus receives the arms of Achilles from Odysseus. Red figure kylix by Douris (c.490 BC).

CHORUS   Earth, mother of all,
                   Mother of Zeus himself,
                    Goddess of mountains,   390
             Ruler of Pactolus, river of gold,
     Blessed lady, mistress of bull-devouring lions,
          I called on you there at Troy,
    When the sons of Atreus directed the full weight
        Of their arrogance against this man   395
         And gave his father's weapons,
            Those wondrous arms,
            To the son of Laertes.

FIRST EPISODE PART 2 (399–487)

399 Friends … The Greek word translated as 'friend' here and at lines 406 and 502 is *xenos*, meaning a stranger, guest or guest-friend (a relationship based on mutual hospitality). This is distinct from the word *philos* (member of the family, close friend, the opposite of enemy (387)) used of Achilles (261), Nestor (415) and Patroclus (428). See note on 507–8.

403 if it might accomplish some criminal end Philoctetes' sketch of Odysseus' methods is strikingly consistent with his portrayal in the Prologue (see Means and ends, page 8).

● Might this disturb Neoptolemus?

404 the greater Ajax Two Ajaxes fought at Troy, though only one is mentioned in this play. The 'greater' Ajax, son of Telamon, was the hero who rescued Achilles' body from the battlefield (see note on The death of Achilles, page 24) and competed unsuccessfully with Odysseus for the arms (see note on lines 61–2). Neoptolemus makes no mention of Ajax's suicide.

410 Tydeus' son Diomedes, who was associated with Odysseus in various daring exploits. Together they raided the Trojan camp in a night adventure (*Iliad x*) and were responsible for the theft of the Palladium, a statuette of Athene, from within the walls of Troy.

411 that bargain Laertes had from Sisyphus The implication is that Laertes paid the bride price for Odysseus' mother *after* she had become pregnant by Sisyphus, thereby getting 'two for the price of one'. Odysseus is elsewhere (in *Ajax*, for example) called the son of Sisyphus as an insult. Sisyphus was notorious for craftiness and was punished in the Underworld for his misdeeds by being forced to push a rock, which kept falling back down, up a hill. However, his craftiness enabled him to cheat even death: having engineered a brief reprieve he was temporarily restored to life, and then refused to return to the Underworld.

415–16 Nestor of Pylos 418 Antilochus Both the aged father (Nestor) and his dutiful son (Antilochus) figure in the *Iliad* as generally sympathetic characters. In *Iliad ix* (52–78) Nestor recommends to Agamemnon sending the embassy to Achilles (see note on line 350) and Antilochus breaks the news of Patroclus' death to Achilles in *Iliad xviii* (16–21). Antilochus' death comes after the end of the *Iliad* while Nestor survives the war and returns home to Pylos (*Odyssey iii*).

PHILOCTETES Friends, it seems you've come here with pain
    that matches mine. Everything you said rings true. I recognise   400
    the work of Odysseus and the sons of Atreus. I know him
    – ready to turn his tongue to any lie and his hand to any
    villainy, if it might accomplish some criminal end. But I am
    surprised at the greater Ajax. If he was there, how could he
    have endured what he saw happening?   405

NEOPTOLEMUS Ajax was dead, friend. If he had been alive they
    would never have stripped me of my armour.

PHILOCTETES What did you say? He is dead, too?

NEOPTOLEMUS Yes. His life is over.

PHILOCTETES A wretched loss! And what about Tydeus' son?   410
    And that bargain Laertes had from Sisyphus? No chance of
    their death – and yet they should never have lived!

NEOPTOLEMUS Oh, no. You can be sure of that. They are alive
    and flourishing even now with the Greek army!

PHILOCTETES And what of my dear old friend, Nestor of   415
    Pylos? Is he still alive? He always used to keep them out of
    trouble through his wise advice.

NEOPTOLEMUS He is not so well now. His son, Antilochus,
    who used to stay close by his side, is dead.

PHILOCTETES Ah, no. Those two are the last people whose   420
    destruction I'd want to hear of. How should we view it, when
    men like that have died – and Odysseus lives on? He, not
    they, should be listed among the dead.

425 it is often the clever ones who trip up Wrestling metaphors are common in describing verbal disputes. In *Knights*, a comedy by Aristophanes, the verbal tricks of Cleon, a popular politician, are described like wrestling moves.

427 Patroclus Philoctetes is shown to have had no news even of the events at Troy described in the *Iliad*, in which the death of Patroclus (*Iliad xvi*) is central.

435 Thersites A minor character who appears briefly and unfavourably in *Iliad ii*. According to some accounts Achilles killed him. The grim catalogue of deaths is perhaps lightened by this mention.

Language
When Aristotle in the *Politics* defines man as a *politikon zōon* (see page 22) he identifies 'speech' as a differentiating factor between man and beast, explaining that it means more than mere animal 'voice':

> Speech, on the other hand, serves to indicate what is useful and what is harmful, and so also what is just and unjust.

Politics 1253a7

In this conversation with Neoptolemus, Philoctetes rediscovers the delights of human conversation: the exchange of news and discussion of shared moral values (see note on Language, page 70).

- How does this exchange a) affect Philoctetes b) further Neoptolemus' aims?

444 We praise the gods, but find them wrong Philoctetes' exclamation, which brings to a close this one-sided exchange of news, suggests moral despair. Philoctetes does not refer explicitly to his own position, but the injustice of his fate is considered by the Chorus later in the play (669–72, see also note on 804 and index – false exits).

- Is Philoctetes' attitude to the gods consistent? (See note on 322.)

445 Son of Oeta's king This way of addressing Philoctetes might remind the audience of the connection with Heracles (see Fathers and sons, page 2).

454 Let's go This is the first in a series of delayed departures (see Another delay …, page 66 and line 516).

Neoptolemus' rhetoric
Before announcing his sudden departure, Neoptolemus claims that the leadership at Troy is corrupt and that he has no place there. His complaints recall those made by his father Achilles against Agamemnon in *Iliad ix* (307–429).

- How sincere does Neoptolemus sound?
- What emotions might be running through his mind at this point?

NEOPTOLEMUS Yes. He is a slippery opponent. But,
    Philoctetes, it is often the clever ones who trip up.   425

PHILOCTETES In the name of the gods, tell me this: where was
    Patroclus while this was going on? He was your father's
    dearest friend.

NEOPTOLEMUS Dead, too. It's a simple lesson: war never
    chooses the wicked, but always the good.   430

PHILOCTETES I bear witness to that. So let me ask you about a
    really worthless man, clever with his tongue and cunning.
    What's happened to him?

NEOPTOLEMUS You mean Odysseus?

PHILOCTETES No. Not him. A man called Thersites. You'd   435
    find he'd talk on and on, though no one wanted to listen to
    him. Do you know if he is still alive?

NEOPTOLEMUS I have never seen him, but from what I've
    heard, yes. He lives on.

PHILOCTETES He would! No, nothing bad ever dies – the gods   440
    take care of that. They somehow take pleasure in keeping
    crime and villainy from Death's door, but they're constantly
    dispatching the good there! What are we to make of this?
    We praise the gods, but find them wrong.

NEOPTOLEMUS Son of Oeta's king, from now on I will keep   445
    my eyes open and stay well away from Troy and the sons of
    Atreus. Where the base man is stronger than the true, and
    good is allowed to rot while the coward is in control, I shall
    not find men I can like. From now on the rocks of Scyros are
    all the home I'll need to keep me happy.   450
    I am going back to the ship now. As for you, son of Poeas,
    fare well, in as far as you can. I hope the gods hear your
    prayer and rid you of your sickness.
    Let's go. We must sail as soon as the god grants us fair
    weather.   455

459 By your father, child Philoctetes' appeal opens with a reference to Neoptolemus' dead father, Achilles.

● What makes this appeal so powerful?

Supplication

460 I beg you as your suppliant Philoctetes speaks of himself as Neoptolemus' suppliant. This means he puts himself under Neoptolemus' protection, imposing on him an *obligation* to respond with help. His words are accompanied by formal gestures of supplication – kneeling and touching the chin or knees. Philoctetes' reference in 472 to Zeus, the suppliants' god, reinforces this appeal. Those who reject suppliants were punishable by Zeus. As at 322f. and despite the words of doubt he has just spoken at 444, Philoctetes seems to retain faith in the righteous powers of the gods.

An alternative appeal

As Philoctetes tries to persuade Neoptolemus he uses words which recall the persuasive talk of Odysseus in the Prologue. Compare Philoctetes' words at 465–7 and 469 with Odysseus' words at 123 and 78–9.

● Are there other examples?
● How different is the *kleos* (see note on page 20) offered by the two older men? Is the tone of their appeals different (see note on lines 91–2)? Which route do you consider more a) glorious b) persuasive?
○ Directors sometimes wish to emphasise parallel scenes. Why? How might this be achieved here?

475–6 the home of Chalcodon on Euboea Chalcodon was an old friend of Heracles. For the island of Euboea, see map on page vi.

476–8 Oeta … Trachis … Spercheius Landmarks of Philoctetes' home.

Appeal by a father

Philoctetes' words recall another famous act of supplication in which Achilles was persuaded to yield up the body of his slain enemy, Hector, by Hector's father King Priam of Troy. Priam's mention of Achilles' own father was a powerful factor. Philoctetes opens his appeal with a reference to Achilles, Neoptolemus' dead father. The most emotive part of the speech is perhaps Philoctetes' reference to Poeas, his own father. Like Philoctetes, the audience do not know if Poeas is alive or dead.

484 how frightening and precarious mortal life is Philoctetes is living proof of his final warning.

○ In staging this speech what physical actions and gestures would strengthen Philoctetes' words?
● Would Neoptolemus' youth and inexperience make him more easily unsettled or more responsive to so powerful an appeal?

PHILOCTETES You are going so soon, child?

NEOPTOLEMUS We need to be by the ships to watch for the
right moment to sail – we can't tell from here.

PHILOCTETES By your father, child. By your mother – by
anyone you love back home, I beg you as your suppliant.   460
Don't leave me here on my own like this. You have seen how
lonely I am, how I live, you have heard how great my troubles
are. Let me come along. I know it's no easy matter to have
something like me on board, but do it. A good man hates to
do wrong. Noble deeds bring glory. Your failure to act would   465
bring dishonour, but if you do this, child, you will earn
yourself a glorious reputation if I get to the land of Oeta
alive.

Come, your suffering will hardly last a day. Be brave. Put me
where you like, but take me: the hold, the bows, the stern –   470
wherever I am going to cause least trouble to the others. Say
'yes', child, I beg you, by Zeus, the suppliant's god. Do what I
ask. I am on my knees to you, though I am a poor, helpless
cripple. Just don't leave me here, alone, far from any trace of
man. Take me safely to your home, or to the home of   475
Chalcodon on Euboea. The journey from there to Oeta will be
quick – to the heights of Trachis and the lovely river
Spercheius. Return me to my dear father – but I fear he is long
since dead. I often asked those who landed here to pass on my
urgent pleas, to get him to send some ship to bring me safely   480
home. He must be dead. Either that or my messengers hurried
on home, not bothering about me. But now I have come to
you, to be my escort and my messenger. Save me. Take pity
on me: see how frightening and precarious mortal life is – one
moment all is fine, the next it's not. [A man without troubles   485
needs to watch out for them. When life is going well, watch
out – disaster strikes when least expected.]

SECOND CHORAL INTERLUDE (488–96)

The Chorus urge Neoptolemus to avoid the anger of the gods and take Philoctetes home. They pick up on his angry words against the sons of Atreus, and suggest that this is a fair return for their crime of abandoning him.

As with the first choral interlude, the words of the Chorus follow Neoptolemus' lead closely, but do they get carried away? There is none of Neoptolemus' deliberate ambiguity (see 505–6) when the Chorus say **take him home**. The question of when and how they were briefed is perhaps significant in gauging the tone here (see note on line 141).

488 Pity him, sir As at 324, the Chorus respond before Neoptolemus and in tones of pity (see Response to Philoctetes' speech, page 22).

496 avoid the anger of the gods This is presumably in response to Philoctetes' act of supplication (see page 34).

The sympathies of the Chorus
- Do you think the words of the Chorus are genuinely sympathetic or are they urging Neoptolemus to continue with the deception?

FIRST EPISODE PART 3 (497–657)

499 close contact with his sickness Neoptolemus' practical comment to his crew also reminds the audience that Philoctetes' wound makes him an unpleasant passenger. Actors would presumably need to sustain this impression throughout the play.

Dramatic irony
Although the audience cannot *know* what Neoptolemus intends to do now, the deliberate ambiguity of his words at 505–6 is a strong reminder of the deceitful nature of the mission and of Neoptolemus' agreement to tell lies. This knowledge affects the way the audience are likely to react to Philoctetes' exclamation of delight at 507: they know more than he does.

- What effect(s) does this use of dramatic irony have?

507–8 You are the kindest of men and your sailors are true friends The man who at 249 described himself as being **without a single friend** (*a-philos*) now includes the Chorus as true friends (*philoi*) and no longer as strangers (*xenoi*) (see notes on 399 and 564).

516 Wait! What's this? Just as Neoptolemus and Philoctetes are about to go into the cave, they are called back by the arrival of two men (see note on 454). Stage entrances and exits are usually signalled by some remark from an actor or the Chorus leader, presumably accompanied by a gesture.

CHORUS   Pity him, sir.
                         His is a tale of struggle,
                            Of troubles hard to bear.   490
                  May no one dear to me ever endure so much.
                  If you hate them, sir, the cruel sons of Atreus,
                          Turn their crime to his advantage.
                          Do as he wishes and take him home.
                       Give him swift, safe passage on our ship   495
                          And avoid the anger of the gods.

NEOPTOLEMUS You are ready to help him now, but make sure
     that you don't change your minds once you've had enough of
     being in close contact with his sickness.

CHORUS Don't worry. We'll give you no cause for reproach.   500

NEOPTOLEMUS Well then, it would be a disgrace if I weren't as
     ready as you to help a friend. If you are happy, let's sail and
     set him on his journey straight away. The ship is ready and it
     won't make any difficulties! All we need is for the gods to
     protect us as we sail away from here, heading for our chosen   505
     destination.

PHILOCTETES The day I've longed for! You are the kindest of
     men and your sailors are true friends. I only wish I could
     express my affection more clearly than in words.
     Let us go, child, but not until we have gone inside and kissed   510
     my home goodbye – my dwelling, it has been no 'home'.
     Then you'll learn how I've lived; how strong I have had to be
     to survive. One look, and I think anyone else would have lost
     heart, but not I. I have had to learn to be content with
     suffering.   515

CHORUS Wait! What's this? There are two men approaching.
     One is from the ship, the other a stranger. Wait to hear from
     them before you go in.

Messenger scenes

At the end of the Prologue Odysseus warned that he would intervene by sending the look-out back in disguise if Neoptolemus seemed **to be taking too long** (131–2).

It was conventional in Greek tragedy for fresh news to be introduced to the plot by a messenger (see page 117). Although usually an incidental character in terms of the plot, the messenger delivered speeches of great intensity and power, often describing events of a violent or shocking nature (for example, the murder of the princess and Creon in *Medea*; the death of Pentheus in *Bacchae*). A messenger might also provide light relief (the guard in *Antigone*; the Corinthian messenger in *Oedipus*).

Odysseus' predicament

Odysseus' whole plan has revolved around the fact that he dare not confront Philoctetes in person: to intervene he has to work by proxy. Earlier versions of the story solved the problem differently. In Aeschylus' version, Philoctetes fails to recognise Odysseus after nearly ten years and simply accepts his story that he is an unknown Greek fugitive. Euripides improved on this improbable scenario by introducing the divine aid of Athene to make Odysseus unrecognisable, as she does in the *Odyssey*. This device, familiar in epic, means the audience know where they stand; Sophocles makes brief use of it in *Ajax* when Athene conceals Odysseus from Ajax, but for this play he creates a more plausible solution.

The use of masks

Three main actors would originally have performed this play (see Introduction to the Greek Theatre, pages 114–17): the protagonist would have taken the role of Philoctetes. The part of Neoptolemus would have been played by the second actor and the third would have played both Odysseus and the Merchant. Additional actors would have taken non-speaking roles. All characters would have worn masks so it was normal and relatively straightforward for different characters to be played by the same actor. This play is unusual in having an exclusively male cast, but often actors would be expected to play roles of different sex as well as age.

Casting the Merchant

It has been suggested that the Merchant should be seen actually as Odysseus disguising his identity and voice (see 1004–5) rather than another member of the crew. Why do *two* men approach at line 516? The theory has attractions. It is entirely in keeping with Odysseus' reputation, particularly in the *Odyssey*, and it would be consistent with Odysseus' character in the rest of this play: his return might be motivated by mistrust of Neoptolemus, a desire to further the action in person, or sheer mischief. On the other hand, the lack of any explicit signalling to this effect would be highly unusual and there is certainly no *need* to view the action as anything other than a conventional messenger scene (see above).

The original production could perhaps have left even the contemporary audience uncertain – a 'meta-theatrical' touch (see page 26)! In the modern theatre, in which it is conventional for different actors to take different roles, the director would have to make a decision when casting the play as to the Merchant's 'true' identity.

Heracles and his bow. Emile-Antoine Bourdelle, 1909.

519 Son of Achilles The Merchant recognises Neoptolemus and addresses only him. Lines 549–55 suggest that Philoctetes does not hear the first part of this exchange.

523–4 sailing home from Troy to Peparethos Such circumstantial details add conviction: a merchant may well have been supplying wine to the forces at Troy. Odysseus shows himself a master of such lies in the *Odyssey* (e.g. *Odyssey xix* 165–202, 221–48).

527 and benefiting in return In material terms, presumably, but perhaps also, to judge from Neoptolemus' response at 532, in the longer term.

530 things are moving fast The main purpose of the Merchant's intervention is to speed Neoptolemus and Philoctetes on their way (see also 543 and 553–4).

531–2 My nobility – if such it be Neoptolemus' words suggest aristocratic grace and disingenuous modesty.

536 Phoenix, and the sons of Theseus Phoenix was Achilles' tutor (see note on 350). The sons of Theseus, a legendary king of Athens, were Acamas and Demophon.

537–8 And are they intending to take me back by force … ? Neoptolemus' words ironically echo those used about his own mission.

546 He and Tydeus' son set out after someone else Odysseus and Diomedes. For Philoctetes' view of this pair see note on lines 410–12.

MERCHANT Son of Achilles, this fellow-trader – who was
    looking after your ship along with a couple of others – was 520
    good enough to tell me where you might be. Our paths have
    crossed, much to my surprise. We just happen to have moored
    in the same place. I'm the skipper of a small crew, sailing
    home from Troy to Peparethos, land of fine wines. When I
    heard from the men that they were all sailing with you, it 525
    didn't seem right to continue my journey without speaking to
    you – and benefiting in return. I suspect you know nothing
    about affairs concerning you closely. The Greeks have got
    new plans for you – and they're not just plans. They're
    already acting on them, and things are moving fast. 530

NEOPTOLEMUS Thanks for your warning, stranger. My
    nobility – if such it be – will ensure that my gratitude lasts.
    Tell me what you have to say; let me know what information
    you have about this new Greek plan.

MERCHANT Your pursuers have already left: the old man, 535
    Phoenix, and the sons of Theseus, with a detachment of ships.

NEOPTOLEMUS And are they intending to take me back by
    force or are they going to talk me into it?

MERCHANT I don't know. I only tell you what I have heard.

NEOPTOLEMUS And it's to gratify the sons of Atreus that 540
    Phoenix and his fellow travellers are going to act with such
    energy?

MERCHANT Not 'going to act' – they're acting now, believe me.

NEOPTOLEMUS How is it that Odysseus wasn't ready to sail
    and bring his own message? Was it fear that held him back? 545

MERCHANT He and Tydeus' son set out after someone else,
    just as I was putting out.

NEOPTOLEMUS Who would Odysseus be sailing after in person?

564 my greatest friend Neoptolemus had said at 386–7 **Anyone who hates Atreus' sons is my friend** (*philos*) so this is a logical development, but it is striking in that Neoptolemus has until now consistently used the term *xenos* of Philoctetes (see note on 399).

A word of caution?

567 Watch what you are doing, boy These lines could also be interpreted as dramatically ironic: is the Merchant cautioning Neoptolemus not to overplay the loyalty?

- What do you think is the tone of Neoptolemus' last words to the Merchant (577–80)?

571–3 This is the man after whom those two ... are sailing In Aeschylus' version, Odysseus, masquerading as a fugitive, lies that Agamemnon is dead and Odysseus has been executed as a criminal – a more obvious way of luring Philoctetes to Troy than by frightening him, which is what the Merchant seems intent on here. The dramatic stage whispers of 549–54 and the artificial build-up of suspense that precede the revelation at 571–3 contribute towards this effect.

- How much of the Merchant's story does Philoctetes hear?
- How is what he hears likely to affect Philoctetes' view of Neoptolemus?

573 They are under oath The resolve of Philoctetes' pursuers is emphasised, as is public knowledge of their intent: it is implicit in 574–6 that Odysseus will lose considerable face if he fails.

The character of the Merchant

- What do we learn of the general character and status of the Merchant?
- How convincing does Sophocles make him?

MERCHANT A man who was... But tell me first who this is? And
whatever you've got to say, say it quietly.   550

NEOPTOLEMUS This man is famous. You'll have heard of him,
stranger. He's Philoctetes.

MERCHANT Ask me no more now. Quick as you can, set sail
and get yourself out of this place.

PHILOCTETES What's he saying, boy? Why are you discussing   555
me? What dark deal is this sea-farer making with you?

NEOPTOLEMUS I'm not sure what he's saying yet. He
must state what he means openly, in front of you and me and
these men here.

MERCHANT Child of Achilles, don't slander me to the army for   560
saying things I shouldn't. I have gained a lot from them in
return for my services. A poor man can do very well.

NEOPTOLEMUS The sons of Atreus are my enemies. This man
is my greatest friend because he hates them too. You have
come to me as a friend. You must not conceal from us   565
anything you have heard.

MERCHANT Watch what you are doing, boy.

NEOPTOLEMUS I have given it careful consideration.

MERCHANT I will hold you responsible for this.

NEOPTOLEMUS Do so, but speak.   570

MERCHANT Very well. This is the man after whom those two I
mentioned, Tydeus' son and the powerful Odysseus, are
sailing. They are under oath and will take him back whether it
requires argument to persuade him or force. All the Achaeans
have heard Odysseus, who is more confident of success than   575
his companion, say so openly.

NEOPTOLEMUS Why are the sons of Atreus suddenly taking
such keen interest in a man they've left so long in exile?
What do they want? Are the gods forcing them? Or is it the
threat of retribution? Those are the powers that fend off evil.   580

The prophecy

Although the Greeks at Troy had a prophet of their own (Calchas), the capture of Helenus by Odysseus in the final stages of the war taught the Greeks how they could bring it to a close. Odysseus was sparing of detail when talking about the prophecy in the Prologue: he simply announced that both Neoptolemus *and the bow* were needed to take Troy (116–17). Here (588) the merchant reveals that **this man** (Philoctetes) is needed – and that he must be persuaded to come. No mention is made of the bow. (See notes on Neoptolemus' 'prophetic words'?, page 62 and The prophecy, page 98.)

Persuasion and force

These words appear frequently in this scene (537–8, 574, 589, 593–4, 599, 605), as they did in the Prologue. They seem most important in terms of the effect they have on Philoctetes.

584–6 caught him ... displayed him ... his fine catch The merchant's picture of Odysseus' humiliating treatment of the captured Helenus makes more vivid the fate Philoctetes is threatened with at 590–4. The point is not lost on Philoctetes, as his words in 606–7 show. (See note on 170 for the recurrent imagery of hunting in this play.)

590–1 he undertook straight away to bring this man for the Achaeans to see As at lines 574–6, Odysseus is represented as boasting publicly; here he goes so far as to stake his life on his ability to bring Philoctetes back.

600 as *his* father did Sisyphus. See note on 411.

Review of the Merchant scene

- How conventional a messenger scene is this (see note on Messenger scenes, page 38)? How does it further the action?
- Why do you think Sophocles chose to use a false messenger rather than a genuine new arrival?
- When you have read through to the end of the first episode (page 45) consider what the dramatic advantages and disadvantages might be of having Odysseus on stage in disguise at this point in the play.

605–6 smooth-talk me into going off ... display me The outraged tone of these words shows how perfectly calculated to provoke a violent reaction this particular aspect of the Merchant's words was.

- Is this a practical demonstration of the lesson, taught to Neoptolemus at line 99, that Philoctetes will not be persuaded?
- What other explanations might there be for so provoking Philoctetes?

MERCHANT I can explain all this to you. Perhaps you have not
heard. There was once a noble prophet, called Helenus,
Priam's son. Odysseus, true to his shameless reputation, went
out on his own by night, and caught him, craftily. Leading
him off in chains, he displayed him to a throng of the   585
Achaeans, his fine catch. Helenus revealed to them many
prophecies and told them that they would never sack Troy's
citadel unless they brought this man from the island where he
currently lives – using argument to persuade him. When
Laertes' son heard the prophet's words he undertook straight   590
away to bring this man for the Achaeans to see. He thought
there was a good chance that he could do this with his
co-operation, but failing that, he'd take the man against his
will. He added that if he was unsuccessful, anyone who wanted
could cut his head off.   595
You've heard it all, boy. I suggest you hurry – you, and
anyone else you care about.

PHILOCTETES Ah, misery! That vicious, cruel man swore he'd
persuade *me* to join the Achaeans? I'd as easily be persuaded
to return from the dead to the light of day – as *his* father did.   600

MERCHANT I don't know anything about that. Anyway, I'm
going back to the ship. May god bring the two of you
whatever is for the best.

PHILOCTETES This is terrible news, boy. That the son of
Laertes should hope, one day, to smooth-talk me into going off   605
in his ship so that he can display me in the middle of the
Greek camp! No! I would rather listen to the snake that
crippled me, my deadliest enemy. But that man could say
anything, has the temerity to do anything. And now I know
that he will be coming here. Child, let's be on our way: put as   610
much sea as possible between Odysseus' ship and us. Let's go.
Speedy action at the right moment brings sleep and rest once
toil is over.

615–18 it's against us … it's against them, too Neoptolemus' caution is at odds with Philoctetes' evident desire to get away fast; it also seems to conflict with the Merchant's clear indication that they should hurry things along. There is the further problem that Neoptolemus' statements seem to be consistent only if he is about to head *away from* Troy to Greece: strangely, he seems more concerned about being blown towards Troy than Philoctetes is.

- What do you think is motivating Neoptolemus here? Is there evidence that Neoptolemus' decision to deceive Philoctetes is weakening?

625 There is a certain herb A reminder of the resourcefulness of the hero. Odysseus conjectured that Philoctetes might have discovered such a plant at lines 42–3. Apart from his bow and arrows, Philoctetes has nothing else he values.

The famous bow

Although Philoctetes has presumably been holding the bow throughout his meeting with Neoptolemus, it is only at this moment that Neoptolemus speaks of it. The significance for the capture of Troy of the **invincible bow** (75) with **deadly arrows** (102) was made clear by Odysseus in the Prologue. In this section it is invested with religious awe because of its associations with the god, Heracles. Heracles was deified because of his services to mankind in ridding the world of monsters, often using this bow.

641 Your words are pious, my child Philoctetes has already spoken of his affection for Neoptolemus, describing him as the kindest of men (507–8). Here, Neoptolemus' scrupulous behaviour prompts further approval, as well as an expression of gratitude perhaps better suited to a prayer of thanksgiving.

- How might these words affect Neoptolemus?

NEOPTOLEMUS Then as soon as this head wind changes direction, we'll set out. At the moment it's against us. 615

PHILOCTETES The wind is always fair when one is fleeing troubles.

NEOPTOLEMUS I know; but it's against them, too.

PHILOCTETES No wind is against robbers with a chance to steal or plunder. 620

NEOPTOLEMUS Then let's go, if you think we should. Get what you need or most want to bring from inside.

PHILOCTETES I only have what I need – and not much of that.

NEOPTOLEMUS Anything we wouldn't have on board?

PHILOCTETES There is a certain herb. It's what I use all the 625
time to soothe the pain from this wound. It brings special relief.

NEOPTOLEMUS Then bring it out. Is there anything else you want to take?

PHILOCTETES Any arrows I may have dropped carelessly. I 630
don't want to leave them for anyone else.

NEOPTOLEMUS Is that the famous bow that you're holding now?

PHILOCTETES This is it – no other – this that I hold in my two hands.

NEOPTOLEMUS May I come closer and take a look? Hold it in 635
my hands and revere it for its divinity?

PHILOCTETES For you, boy, this, and anything else I have that can help you.

NEOPTOLEMUS I long to take it, but my desire is like this: if it is
lawful, I would like to; if not, then let it go. 640

PHILOCTETES Your words are pious, my child, and it *is* lawful:
you alone have granted me the gift of looking upon the light
of this day, of seeing the land of Oeta, my aged father and my
loved ones; you have freed me from my enemies and set me
beyond their reach. 645

649–50 It was for an act of kindness that I once won it, too
Philoctetes lit the funeral pyre which enabled Heracles to die (see
Background to the story, page v). He was rewarded with the bow of
Heracles and consequent *kleos* (see note on *kleos*, page 20). Philoctetes
equates Neoptolemus' action in releasing him from his island prison
with his own act of deliverance in lighting the pyre: by holding the
bow Neoptolemus begins to win the **glorious reputation** promised
him by Philoctetes at 467.

Friendship
651 My spirits lighten A more literal translation would be '*I feel the
lifting of a burden*': Neoptolemus' first words of friendship spoken
directly to Philoctetes (see 564) are simple and effective.
○ At what point(s) should the bow change hands?

Take courage. You may handle this bow and arrows and
then return them to their giver. You will be able to claim to
be one of the only mortals who has touched this bow –
because of your virtue. It was for an act of kindness that I
once won it, too.   650

NEOPTOLEMUS My spirits lighten as I look at you and accept you
as my friend. A person who knows how to deal kindly when
kindly treated can become something dearer than any
possession – a friend.

Please, go inside.   655

PHILOCTETES I'll show you the way. My sickness makes me crave
your constant presence.

FIRST *STASIMON* (658–728)

A *stasimon* is the term given to the choral song that comes at the end of an episode.

Philoctetes and Neoptolemus go into the cave leaving the Chorus alone.

The Chorus try to find a mythological parallel for Philoctetes' suffering, but the best they can come up with is the story of Ixion (see note below). Where is the justice in Philoctetes' punishment? The Chorus wonder at Philoctetes' fortitude and dwell once again on the cruelty of his enforced isolation from other human beings.

Ixion

658–9 There's a tale / I've heard told The Chorus in tragedy often introduce mythological parallels as a way of commenting on the action (e.g. *Antigone* 944ff., *Medea* 1283–9). Here, the style is allusive: the audience were expected to pick up the reference. Some may have seen more parallels than are explicitly mentioned.

Ixion threw his prospective father-in-law, with whom he had had some disagreement about the bride price, into a pit filled with burning coals. This murder was considered so beyond pardon that only Zeus was prepared to accept him as his **suppliant** (see note on Supplication, page 34). Ixion went on to abuse Zeus' hospitality by attempting to seduce Hera, Zeus' wife. He was foiled by Zeus who substituted a cloud for the goddess and then punished Ixion by chaining him to a perpetually spinning wheel.

- Ixion's punishment might seem just; is there any justice in Philoctetes' punishment?

662 Cronus' son Zeus was son of Cronus (Saturn) who was son of Ge and Uranus (see note on line 388).

664–5 But I have never heard of / Or seen Philoctetes' fate defies comparison even with stories from mythology. The contrast with 658–9 emphasises the impact of witnessing Philoctetes' suffering at first hand.

675–6 How has he held on to a life / So full of tears … ? This echoes thoughts expressed by Philoctetes himself in 511–15.

Isolation

Many of the themes in this *stasimon* have been touched on earlier in the play. The pity the Chorus expressed for Philoctetes' lack of human contact in the *parodos* is developed here, with particular reference to the absence of anyone who might hear his cries and communicate with him.

CHORUS There's a tale
I've heard told, but never witnessed myself,
Of how a man once drew near   660
The bed of Zeus.
Cronus' son bound him with chains
To the spinning rim of a wheel.

But I have never heard of
Or seen   665
Any mortal
Who has met with a more bitter fate
Than this man's.

He harmed no one,
Cheated no one,   670
Was fair in dealing with others.
His destruction is unjust.

Wonder fills me.
How? How?
How has he held on to a life   675
So full of tears,
As he listened
Alone
To the roar of the waves
Breaking around him?   680

He had no neighbour
Except himself,
Couldn't visit
Because he couldn't walk.
There was no one near to whom he could go   685
With whom he could share his troubles,
Weeping aloud,
Exchanging cries
For his gnawing,
Bloody pain.   690

691–714 The Chorus have perhaps learned some of the small details here by watching and listening to Philoctetes: his use of herbs (625), the way he has to move to find food (300–3), the spasmodic nature of the pain (see note on Philoctetes' fit, page 56).

○ How do these lines help an actor thinking about how Philoctetes should move?

695 But no one was there to offer relief Philoctetes' isolation means he lacks not only anyone with whom he can communicate, but also medical help, assistance in moving around and gathering food, and the benefits of settled agriculture providing food and wine.

704–5 no share of the produce / We cultivate to sell The Chorus include themselves in the collective group of civilised men who enjoy a settled pattern of agriculture producing a surplus – a social structure from which Philoctetes is extraordinary in being excluded. (See Aristotle's definition of man, page 22.)

710 No delight from a drink of wine Ironically, Lemnos is elsewhere celebrated for its wine (*Iliad vii* (467) and *viii* (232); Aristophanes' *Peace* (1162)).

The injustice of Philoctetes' punishment
● Is the audience or reader able to respond with any more understanding than the Chorus to Philoctetes' fate?
● Do you think there are lessons an audience might learn from looking at the fate of Philoctetes?

When an attack came on,
His ulcerated foot,
Savage with pain,
Seeped hot, bloody pus;
But no one was there to offer relief   695
With soothing herbs
Gathered from the bounteous earth.

He would creep this way and that,
Crawling sometimes
Like a child without his loving nurse   700
To wherever he might get food,
When the soul-biting anguish loosed its grip.

His food was not sown in the fruitful earth;
He has no share of the produce
We cultivate to sell,   705
Only what he could get
With his swift bow and winged arrows
To feed his stomach.

Miserable life!
No delight from a drink of wine   710
For ten years.
Continually making his way
To the pools of water
He'd learned to search out.

The stasimon changes tone and ends on an uplifting note: Philoctetes has found somebody to deliver him and return him home to Malis, the place of Heracles' deification.

715–28 But now … sacred fire Is the change of tone prompted by the return of Neoptolemus and Philoctetes from the cave?

716 He will find happiness and again be great The Chorus' words are confusing: they speak of Philoctetes' future happiness (in returning home), but why will he *again* be great? There is a tension between a happy life at home and winning a reputation for greatness (*kleos* – see note on page 20), explored in *Iliad ix*. Philoctetes already has some claim to fame, firstly as the man who mastered the bow of Heracles and now as a man who survived ten years in isolation, but it is surely by going to Troy that Philoctetes' undying glory will be secured.

717–18 a child / From a noble family The nobility of Neoptolemus' birth is a recurrent theme (see 89–90, 343, 531–2 and note on Nobility, page 64).

● How noble does Neoptolemus appear at this point in the play?

722–5 Malis … Spercheius … Oeta These landmarks of Philoctetes' home (see 476–8) recall the scene of his fateful encounter with Heracles.

726 A man with a bronze shield This reference to Heracles with a shield refers to his cult in Athens as a hoplite (heavy-armed infantry) warrior.

728 his father's sacred fire Heracles' father is Zeus, whose sacred fire is formed from the bolts of lightning with which he strikes down evildoers. Zeus is often depicted in art hurling a lightning bolt.

Review of the first *stasimon*

Throughout the play the Chorus are involved in and contribute significantly towards the action of the play (e.g. at 488–96, 1104–5). It is therefore appropriate to ask questions about their sympathies and motivation. However, the traditional roles of the Chorus and actors were different: choral singing and dancing may serve as an interlude, reflecting on, reinforcing, or moving beyond the emotions and themes of the preceding episode. This *stasimon* is placed half-way through the drama. It both looks back to the past sufferings of Philoctetes and examines the present opportunities for escape from them. As will be seen, it foreshadows the eventual outcome of the drama, but gives nothing away.

● Analyse the prevailing themes and emotions developed in this *stasimon*.

● How might the sympathies and understanding of the audience be affected by the Chorus' words?

But now, leaving this behind, 715
He will find happiness and again be great.
He has met a child
From a noble family
Who is taking him home,
After all this time, 720
In his seafaring ship,
To Malis, haunt of nymphs.

His homeland,
By the banks of Spercheius
Where, beyond Oeta's heights, 725
A man with a bronze shield
Came close to the gods,
Brilliant in his father's sacred fire.

SECOND EPISODE (729–838)

Philoctetes' fit

731 *A, a, a, a!* In the original Greek a number of different sounds were used to indicate Philoctetes' cries of pain. These have simply been transliterated. Neoptolemus' words at 740–1 suggest that the cries at 731 and 739 are repressed; the sounds gain in intensity as the disease establishes its grip on Philoctetes (747ff.).

Neoptolemus' reaction

The exchange between Neoptolemus and Philoctetes is swift and intense. The pattern of *stichomythia* (where alternating lines of Greek iambic trimeters – the metre of most of the dialogue – are given to the two characters speaking) is upset: in one line of Greek there are four separate exchanges (753–6)! This increase in pace perhaps helps to characterise Neoptolemus' bewilderment.

- What do you think Philoctetes is asking Neoptolemus at line 753? (Line 791 perhaps refers back to this exchange.)

NEOPTOLEMUS Come then, if you are willing.
Why are you suddenly silent? What has made you freeze like this? 730

PHILOCTETES *A, a, a, a!*

NEOPTOLEMUS What is it?

PHILOCTETES Nothing serious. Come on, child.

NEOPTOLEMUS Is your sickness causing you pain?

PHILOCTETES No, I'm all right. I think it's easing up now. Gods! 735

NEOPTOLEMUS Why are you crying out to the gods like this?

PHILOCTETES To ask them to be gentle to me, to come and
save me.
A, a, a, a!

NEOPTOLEMUS What's wrong with you? Don't keep quiet about it 740
like this, tell me! You seem to be in some sort of trouble.

PHILOCTETES It's all over for me, child. I can't keep it hidden
from you.
Attatai!
It goes through me, through me. Ah, misery. It's all over, I'm 745
finished, child. I'm being eaten alive.
Papai! Apappapai! Papa! Papa! Papa! Papai!
By the gods, child, if you have a sword to hand, strike at my
foot. Cut it off, quick as you can. Don't spare my life. Go on,
boy. 750

NEOPTOLEMUS What is it that's suddenly making you scream and
cry out like this?

PHILOCTETES Do you know, child?

NEOPTOLEMUS What?

PHILOCTETES Don't you know, boy? 755

NEOPTOLEMUS What do you want? I *don't* know.

PHILOCTETES How can you not know?
Pappapappapai!

NEOPTOLEMUS The burden of this sickness is terrible.

772 And if, during this time, *they* come 'They' are Odysseus and Diomedes. Philoctetes heard the Merchant's warning at 571–4 that they were on a mission to take him back to Troy. Philoctetes seems more concerned about the bow than about himself. His dependence upon it for protection is implicit, but he is also concerned that Neoptolemus should not leave him (762, 791, 813). Entrusting the bow to Neoptolemus increases Philoctetes' dependency upon him and Neoptolemus' moral obligations in return. Philoctetes reminds him of these in 775 (see note on Supplication, page 34).

777–8 may fortune come with it
● What do you think Neoptolemus means here?

The bow

As Philoctetes passes the bow to Neoptolemus for a second time (see page 48) he warns Neoptolemus to show reverence: neither of the bow's previous owners, Heracles and Philoctetes, have enjoyed good fortune in life, though they have been honoured and helped by their possession of the bow.

782 Gods, grant these prayers Neoptolemus makes an additional prayer for a safe voyage.
Compare what he says here with his words at 502–6.

785 A, a, a, a! A second wave of pain attacks Philoctetes.

789 Foot! Philoctetes cries out to his foot. He frequently addresses inanimate objects and parts of his body directly (see notes on Language, pages 32 and 70).

PHILOCTETES Yes, terrible. Unspeakable. Pity me! 760

NEOPTOLEMUS What should I do?

PHILOCTETES Don't take fright and betray me. This happens
from time to time: the disease comes and goes, moving on
when it's taken its fill.

NEOPTOLEMUS Poor, poor wretch! All these sufferings make 765
you wretched indeed! Would you like me to hold you,
comfort you?

PHILOCTETES No, don't! But take my bow, just as you asked to
before. Take it until the present attack subsides. Keep it safe
and guard it. Sleep takes hold of me whenever the pain lets 770
up. Until then, there's no release. You must let me sleep in
peace. And if, during this time, *they* come, then I charge you
by the gods not to give it up to them, not willingly, not
unwillingly, whatever they try. If you do, you will destroy
both yourself and me: I am your suppliant. 775

NEOPTOLEMUS Have no fear about my intentions. No one will
hold this bow except you and me. Pass it to me, and may
fortune come with it.

PHILOCTETES Here. Take it, boy. Show reverence to turn aside
the jealousy of the gods. Don't let the same troubles visit you 780
as did me and the one who had this bow before me.

NEOPTOLEMUS Gods, grant these prayers to us both. Grant us a
fair and easy voyage to our destination: to wherever heaven
judges right and our mission tends.

PHILOCTETES *A, a, a, a!* 785
I'm afraid, boy, your prayers may be in vain. The blood is
flowing again, dark and thick from deep down. I expect worse.
Papai! Pheu! Papai! Pa–
Foot! How you torment me!
It's coming! It's coming closer! Help me! 790
Now you understand. Don't run away!
Attatai!

Revenge

At the height of his agony, Philoctetes' thoughts return to his oppressors. Here and elsewhere (290–1, 322–3) his curses express the desire that they should experience his suffering: he seems unable to imagine a worse – or more just – punishment for them.

Death

Philoctetes' cry **Omoi, moi!** (799) seems to mark a change of tone. Philoctetes goes on to appeal to Death, frequently personified in poetry (as is Sleep at 839f). At 319 he described his life on Lemnos as a slow death, but this is the first time we hear him so full of despair that he wants to die. There is something pathetic in the suggestion that this daily prayer has been unanswered.

801–2 summon up the fires of Lemnos and burn my body here

Philoctetes asks Neoptolemus to perform for him the role that he performed for Heracles as a youth (see Background to the story, page v and note on 649–50). Instead of the prepared funeral pyre, he refers to the natural fires of Lemnos from the volcano Moschylos.

Philoctetes' innocence

804 I thought I was acting rightly Philoctetes' act of lighting the pyre to release Heracles from the agony of the poisoned robe which was consuming him (see Background to the story, page v) seemed to be one of mercy and one for which he was rewarded with the weapons of Heracles. His innocence, which is emphasised elsewhere, in particular by the Chorus (see pages 50–2), makes his subsequent fate seem unjust.

- Like Neoptolemus, Philoctetes is faced in youth with a difficult decision about how to act. In what ways are the two situations either similar or different?

808 Child, where are you? Philoctetes' momentary panic reflects the fears he has already expressed (762, 791). It also perhaps motivates his wish for some stronger form of reassurance.

The pledge

821 Neoptolemus offers Philoctetes his hand as a sign of trust.

- What precisely does he promise?

I only wish, my Ithacan visitor, that you could feel this
agony shooting through your breast.

Pheu! Papai! Papai! Papai! 795

And you two commanders, Agamemnon and Menelaus, what
if you could take my place, feed this infection for as long as I
have?

Omoi, moi! Death! Death! How is it that every day I call on
you like this, but you can never come? 800

Child, noble child, take me; summon up the fires of Lemnos
and burn my body here, noble one. I did this once, too – for
the son of Zeus. In return I received the weapon which you
now keep safe. I thought I was acting rightly.

Well, what do you say, boy? 805

What's your answer?

Why don't you speak?

Child, where are you?

NEOPTOLEMUS I've been feeling your pain, upset by your
troubles all this time. 810

PHILOCTETES Oh, child! Take courage. Its attacks are sharp, but
they are quickly over.

Please, I beg you, don't leave me on my own.

NEOPTOLEMUS Don't worry, we'll wait.

PHILOCTETES You will? 815

NEOPTOLEMUS Be sure of it.

PHILOCTETES I feel it's not right to place you under oath, child.

NEOPTOLEMUS Just as it would be wrong for me to go without
you.

PHILOCTETES Give me your hand on it. 820

NEOPTOLEMUS My hand says I will wait.

PHILOCTETES Now, over there. Take me over there.

NEOPTOLEMUS Where do you mean?

PHILOCTETES Up.

NEOPTOLEMUS What are you trying to do now? Why are you 825
looking up at the sky?

PHILOCTETES Let me go! Let me go!

NEOPTOLEMUS Let you go where?

Review of the second episode

This scene gives us a sudden insight into the nature and intensity of Philoctetes' disease. The initial impression of Philoctetes' state formed by Neoptolemus, his crew and the audience is shown to represent only part of the picture.

- What is the dramatic effect of delaying the full impact of Philoctetes' suffering in this way?
- Many graphic details of the disease are given in the course of this scene. How coherent a picture do they present? How is the impression of Philoctetes' intimate familiarity with the sickness conveyed? Do you find this scene dramatically convincing? Is it more likely to alienate an audience or play on their sympathies?

FIRST *COMMUS* (839–83)

A *commus* is a lyric dialogue between Chorus and actor, usually one in which some emotional crisis comes to a head. (In this play, it takes the place of a second *stasimon*.) In both *Antigone* and *Oedipus* there are two *commoi*: the first in each case is used in expressing conflicting views between Chorus and actor, as here; in the second, the Chorus respond with sympathy to the events on stage (see note on page 78).

839 As Philoctetes collapses on the ground, the Chorus begin to sing to Sleep. The soft opening words invite Sleep to heal Philoctetes' suffering and offer welcome relief from the emotional intensity of the preceding scene, but this quickly changes to a more urgent note as the Chorus tell Neoptolemus to act (847–54).

Neoptolemus' 'prophetic words'?

Lines 855–9 are Greek hexameters, the usual metre for epic poetry, not tragedy. They are also used in oracular responses. Here, the metre makes Neoptolemus' utterance sound inspired.

- Neoptolemus was told by Odysseus at 113 that Philoctetes' bow was required for the capture of Troy. Further information from the Merchant (587–8) placed the emphasis on Philoctetes himself and made no specific mention of the weapons. Is this source of information sufficient to explain Neoptolemus' words or does his utterance seem inspired?
- How might attention be drawn to these words in production?
- How do the Chorus respond to them?

PHILOCTETES Will you let me go!

NEOPTOLEMUS I refuse to leave you. 830

PHILOCTETES You'll kill me if you touch me.

NEOPTOLEMUS All right. I'll let you go, if you are feeling better.

PHILOCTETES Earth! Take me as I am, ready for death. This
evil no longer lets me stay upright.

NEOPTOLEMUS It looks like he'll soon be asleep. See, his head 835
is nodding. His whole body is soaked with sweat. A vein of black
blood has burst in his heel. Let's leave him to rest, friends. Let
him sleep.

CHORUS   Sleep, innocent of pain,
                   Sleep, innocent of hurt, 840
              Breathe over us, lord, soft breathed
                        Contentment,
                   And sweet happiness.
                    Let your radiance
                   Fill his eyes, as now. 845
                   Come, Healer, come.

              Child, consider where you stand,
                      Your next step,
                    What do you think?
                   You see how things are. 850
                   Why are we waiting?
                       Swift action
                   At the right moment
                   Is wise and effective.

NEOPTOLEMUS He can't hear us, but I know this: 855
Our hunt for the bow will fail if we leave him here, sailing away.
          He is the one the god commanded us fetch,
                  the garland of honour is his.
To boast of a deed half-done, to lie, brings only shame and disgrace.

CHORUS   These are matters for the god, child. 860
              When you answer me next,
              Speak softly, child, softly.

Chorus and Neoptolemus

This is not the first time the Chorus have prompted Neoptolemus to take control (see *parodos*, 139–50, 231–4, 488–96).

- How would you characterise the relationship between Neoptolemus and his crew?
- Which words best describe the tone of their language here: *secretive, confident, awkward, sinister, practical, subordinate*?

Philoctetes asleep

In lines 285–9 Philoctetes describes to Neoptolemus how he was tricked while sleeping on the shore by Odysseus, who left without waking him. Neoptolemus finds himself in precisely the same situation with the opportunity to repeat Odysseus' action. The parallels of the situation do not escape Philoctetes who draws a bitter comparison at 889–91.

THIRD EPISODE (884–1110)

886 Light after sleep!

- What is suggested by Philoctetes' use of the word **light**?

Nobility

891–2 your nature is noble, child, true to your nobility The word for noble here is *eu-genēs*, meaning 'well-born'. At 919–20 Philoctetes states that in **helping an honourable man** Neoptolemus' behaviour is true to his birth. Philoctetes judges him by the standard of how his father, Achilles, would have behaved, but there seems to be the further assumption that nobility is somehow hereditary.

- Is this a satisfactory way of defining 'nobility' of action?
- Are the standards by which Neoptolemus judges himself at 917–18 and 921 any different from those of Philoctetes?

894–5 Help me up – do it yourself, child Philoctetes asks for help in standing after his attack, but it is a number of lines before he finally stands, dispensing with Neoptolemus' services as he does so (908).

- What are the actors doing during this time? Why do you think there is so much focus on this action in the text?

Sleep brings no rest
to the sick:
The eyes are sharp   865
And quick to see.
Look out for a way
To do it in secret.
You know what I mean:
If your plans for him   870
Don't change... well, the wise
Might foresee difficulties and pain.

The winds are in our favour, child.
His eyes are closed. He lies
Stretched out in the dark, helpless,   875
In a deep, untroubled sleep.
His hands and feet are limp,
Like someone lying dead.
Does what you're saying
Suit the moment? Think!   880
As I understand it, boy,
The most effective course
Is not to cause alarm.

NEOPTOLEMUS Be quiet! Keep your wits about you. His eyes
are opening. He's lifting his head.   885

PHILOCTETES Light after sleep! I had not expected this – that
these strangers would stay and watch over me. Child, I never
thought you'd show such pity for my troubles, waiting
patiently by my side, looking after me. There was no
patience or tolerance from those gallant commanders, the   890
sons of Atreus! But your nature is noble, child, true to your
nobility. You've had your fill of my shouting and the stench,
but you've made light of it all. And now, since I can forget
my trouble and there's some respite, lift me. Help me up – do
it yourself, child. Then, as soon as the weakness goes, we can 895
set off to the ship and sail without delay.

Another delay…

Apart from the detour to the cave to collect Philoctetes' belongings (510, 621–2, see also note on 454) Philoctetes and Neoptolemus have been stopped from leaving for the ship twice: at line 516 by the arrival of the Merchant and again by the attack of Philoctetes' sickness at the start of the second episode (line 729). Here they are delayed for a third time – on this occasion because of Neoptolemus.

909 *Papai!* This word of anguish perhaps points to the parallel between Philoctetes' physical pain and Neoptolemus' mental agony. Throughout this episode Neoptolemus repeats that this is not a sudden pang of guilt, but a growing feeling of revulsion for his role as deceiver (914, 921–2, see also 931–2).

● How could the progression of this feeling of revulsion be brought out by an actor? At what point do you feel it began?

915 You're disgusted by my infection Philoctetes misunderstands Neoptolemus' disgust in a manner consistent with previous experience: he has anticipated a reaction of physical repulsion throughout (469–71, 892, 904–6); he has no other suspicions.

919–20 your father Achilles' gallant offer of protection to Calchas in *Iliad i* (84–21) is characteristic.

NEOPTOLEMUS The sight of you fills me with a joy I hadn't
hoped for. Your pain is gone, and you're alive, still breathing.
Given your state, you looked as if you might be dead.
Now, up you get. Or, if you prefer, these men will lift you.   900
There'll be no shirking from the job now that you and I are
decided about what we should do.

PHILOCTETES Well said, boy. Help me up, as you suggest. But
leave your men be. That way they won't suffer from the
terrible smell before they need to. They'll have enough to put   905
up with, living on board ship with me.

NEOPTOLEMUS So be it. Up you get. Hold on to me.

PHILOCTETES Don't worry. I can get up; I've done this before!

NEOPTOLEMUS *Papai!* What do I do next?

PHILOCTETES What is it, boy? What were you going to say?   910

NEOPTOLEMUS I don't know how to express my confusion.

PHILOCTETES What are you confused about? Child, don't talk
like this.

NEOPTOLEMUS I find myself so deep in this feeling.

PHILOCTETES You're disgusted by my infection – and this has   915
persuaded you not to take me on board ship any longer?

NEOPTOLEMUS Everything causes disgust when a man forsakes
his own nature and does something beneath him.

PHILOCTETES But you are not doing or saying anything your
father would not have done in helping an honourable man.   920

NEOPTOLEMUS I shall be exposed as base. This is what I've
been agonising over all this time.

PHILOCTETES It's what you are saying not what you're doing
that makes me afraid.

925 Zeus The force of Neoptolemus' state of confusion is emphasised by his appeal to Zeus here.

926 what I should not have concealed That Troy is their intended destination.

927 the shameful words I have spoken
● Is Neoptolemus referring to specific words? If so, to what?

Neoptolemus' confession
Neoptolemus' statement that he must take Philoctetes to Troy is simple and direct. Philoctetes' interruptions make it difficult for Neoptolemus to explain, and no reference is made to the oracle.

944 We are ruled by the power of necessity
949–50 It is right and in our interest to listen to those in authority
These lines sound flat – like phrases Neoptolemus is repeating from someone else. They are reminiscent of what Odysseus has said in the Prologue. The extent to which Philoctetes is convinced by Neoptolemus' words is made clear by the violence of his response.

● Consider Neoptolemus' two statements. What do you think he means by **the power of necessity**? Do you think he sees it as the same as or different from the voice of **those in authority**?

Philoctetes' reaction
This explosive speech begins with three vocatives: more literally, Philoctetes calls Neoptolemus **fire, every terror, most hated artifice of all terrible/clever deeds**. Sophocles also uses this technique in *Oedipus* (380–1) to show anger.

● What ideas are suggested by Sophocles' choice of images here?

NEOPTOLEMUS Zeus, what shall I do? Will I be caught in the   925
wrong twice? Firstly, for what I should not have concealed
and secondly, for the shameful words I have spoken.

PHILOCTETES If my wits have not left me, it looks as if this
man is about to betray me and to sail off, leaving me behind.

NEOPTOLEMUS I'm not going to leave you. It's where I'm   930
sending you that is causing the pain. This is what I've been
agonising over all this time.

PHILOCTETES What are you saying, child? I don't understand.

NEOPTOLEMUS I'll not keep it secret from you.
You must sail to Troy, to the Greeks and to the army of   935
Agamemnon and Menelaus.

PHILOCTETES Ah, no. What are you saying?

NEOPTOLEMUS Don't be upset until you've learned…

PHILOCTETES Learned what? What are your plans for me?

NEOPTOLEMUS Most importantly, to save you from this   940
misery. Then, to go with you and lay waste the plains of
Troy.

PHILOCTETES So this is your real intention?

NEOPTOLEMUS We are ruled by the power of necessity. Don't
be angry listening to me.   945

PHILOCTETES Ah, wretched! I am destroyed. I have been
betrayed. What have you done to me, stranger? Quickly, give
me back my bow.

NEOPTOLEMUS I can't. It is right and in our interest to
listen to those in authority.   950

PHILOCTETES You leave a trail like fire! Terrifying, through
and through! A hateful, clever, scheming worker of evil!
Look what you've done to me! How you've deceived me! Do
you feel no shame as you look at me? I am in your power,
I'm your suppliant, you wretch! By taking my bow you have   955
deprived me of life. Give it back, I beg of you. Give it back,

Language

Realising that he is once again the victim of human deceit and betrayal, Philoctetes appeals to the beasts and inanimate landscape (960), in particular his cave (976). Some idiosyncrasies of Philoctetes' speech were noted previously (see note on 277). Here we again begin to see how Philoctetes has survived isolation without losing the power of 'speech' (see Aristotle's definition of man, page 22). At 789, during his fit, Philoctetes cried out to his foot and in 799 to Death personified. As he feels increasingly isolated, his use of such vocatives – to elemental forces (earth 833, light 886), parts of his body (1038), his bow (1164), his cave (976, 1111), the physical landscape (960, 1018) and its inhabitants (960, 1124) – intensifies as he is driven back to his old 'companions'.

957–8 don't rob me of my life The Greek word for 'bow' (*bios*) and 'life' (*bios*) are very similar (they are pronounced slightly differently in Greek). Sophocles twice plays on this pun (see also 1348).

966–7 parade it in front of the Argives! Philoctetes' words recall the Merchant's tale of Odysseus' capture of Helenus (582–6) and his plans for Philoctetes. The fear of being humiliated in front of the Greeks (Argives) seems to haunt Philoctetes (605–7).

968 in killing me

● Is Philoctetes exaggerating or is this accusation justifiable?

973 Give it back! Be like yourself again! Philoctetes seems suddenly filled with hope that Neoptolemus may revert to being the man he seemed before.

● Trace the shifts of tone in this speech. How many times does Philoctetes change tack? Is he being manipulative?

975 No response? This is not the first time that Philoctetes has to prompt Neoptolemus to speak (see 250, 910). However, here he does not respond. At 1098–9 Philoctetes asks Neoptolemus to break his silence.

○ What might an actor playing Neoptolemus be doing during this time?

● How much movement do you think there should be from Philoctetes during his speech?

The Chorus

Once again, the Chorus speak first, prompting a response from Neoptolemus (see Response to Philoctetes' speech, page 22 and note on 488), but they make it clear that the decision must be his.

● How and why has the role of the Chorus changed in this third episode?

I beg you as your suppliant, child. By your father's gods, don't
rob me of my life. Oh, misery! He no longer answers me, but
looks away – as if he'll never let it go!

Bays! Headlands! Beasts who've shared my mountain life!   960
Craggy rocks! It is to you I cry out. You are the companions
I've grown used to. I have no one else to talk to. Do you see
what this boy, this son of Achilles, has done to me? He swore
he would take me home, but he's taking me to Troy. He
offered his right hand, but has taken my bow – the sacred bow   965
of Heracles, son of Zeus. And he wants to parade it in front
of the Argives! Oh, it is a mighty opponent he has captured
and carried off by force! He doesn't know that in killing me
he is slaying a mere corpse, a wisp of smoke, a phantom. He
would never have taken me if I had my strength. Even like   970
this he couldn't catch me – except by trickery! But now here
I am: wretched victim of his deceit. What should I do?
Give it back! Be like yourself again!
What do you say?
No response? Then I'm finished, a wretched victim.   975
My two-mouthed cave, I return to you again, but this time
I have no weapons, no means of finding food.
Alone in this cave I shall wither away. Without that bow I'll
not kill a bird on the wing or a mountain beast. I myself will
provide a feast for those I used to eat with my pitiful dead   980
body. The animals I hunted will be my hunters now. I shall
pay for their deaths in death, the pitiful victim of one who
seemed to know nothing of evil.
A curse on you – but not yet, not until I know if you might
change your mind back again. If not, may your death be slow   985
and painful.

CHORUS What should we do? Master, it is up to you now: do we
  sail or do we listen to what this man has to say?

aporia

In Neoptolemus' next three speeches he expresses his *aporia* – his confusion and uncertainty how to respond – torn between pity for Philoctetes and loyalty towards Odysseus and the Greek army. This is the fourth time he has asked what he should do next (761, 909, 925, 994).

The meeting of Odysseus and Philoctetes

Since the opening of the play and Odysseus' arrival on Lemnos there has been tense anticipation of the possibility of the two enemies meeting face to face (see note on Dramatic tension, page 2), heightened by the drama of the Merchant scene. It was unusual to have a character appear (or reappear) on stage without their arrival being signalled. Here, surprise is of the essence – and so is timing (Odysseus springs out of hiding mid-way through Neoptolemus' line).

- Was Neoptolemus about to return the bow as Odysseus' words at 1002 suggest?

Odysseus must have witnessed some, at least, of the preceding scene, since he would not reveal himself unless he knew that Philoctetes was unarmed. (See note on Staging Odysseus' return, page 94.)

1004–5 Is that the voice of Odysseus I hear? Philoctetes instantly recognises the voice of his enemy, as if he has been waiting for it since hearing the Merchant's news (571–3). At line 998 Philoctetes had guessed that someone had influenced or *schooled* Neoptolemus: he is quick to make the further connection that Odysseus is behind the deception.

1011 Give it back! Give me the bow, boy! Neoptolemus is caught between Odysseus and Philoctetes both demanding the bow (Philoctetes at 956, 973, 1011 and Odysseus at 1003).

- ○ Consider the staging at this point in the play, perhaps using a simple sketch: what is the position of Neoptolemus in relation to the two older men?
- For how long is Neoptolemus silent this time? (See note on 975.)

Force

Odysseus' objection to the use of force is no longer relevant now that Philoctetes no longer has his bow.

- Which do you think outrages Philoctetes more at 1015 and 1019: the idea of being *forced* off the island, or the irony that the man who abandoned him on Lemnos might make him leave it?

1018 Mighty flames of Hephaestus! Hephaestus was god of fire and blacksmiths, and was associated with volcanoes (see 801). In *Iliad i*, Hephaestus describes how Zeus punished him for defending his

NEOPTOLEMUS A terrible sense of pity for this man has overwhelmed me. Not a sudden feeling, but one which has been growing. 990

PHILOCTETES In the name of the gods, show compassion. Don't let people reproach you for deceiving me.

NEOPTOLEMUS Oh, what am I going to do? It would have been better if I had never left Scyros. Everything around me oppresses me... 995

PHILOCTETES It is not you who are bad. It seems you've come here schooled in shamelessness by men who are evil. Hand over to others better suited. Sail away – and leave me my weapons. 1000

NEOPTOLEMUS What should we do, men?

ODYSSEUS What are you doing, you utter wretch? Come and give the bow to me.

PHILOCTETES Oh, no! Who is it? Is that the voice of Odysseus I hear? 1005

ODYSSEUS Yes it's me, Odysseus, you can be sure, before your very eyes.

PHILOCTETES No! I've been betrayed. I am ruined. *He's* the one who's caught me and separated me from my bow.

ODYSSEUS I and no other. Rest assured. On that we agree. 1010

PHILOCTETES Give it back! Give me the bow, boy!

ODYSSEUS That he will never do, not even if he wants to. Moreover, you must come along with your weapons. If not, you will be brought by force.

PHILOCTETES Is there no limit to your shamelessness? These 1015 men are going to use force to take me away?

ODYSSEUS If you don't come willingly.

PHILOCTETES Land of Lemnos! Mighty flames of Hephaestus! It is unendurable that this man should force me away from you. 1020

ODYSSEUS Know this: these things have been decided by Zeus. Zeus rules this land. It is Zeus I serve.

Odysseus' justification

At 1021–2 Odysseus invokes Zeus as justification for his actions, causing Philoctetes further outrage.

- Consider the tone of Odysseus' responses in lines 1021–31. Is he, despite the opinion he expressed at 99 that Philoctetes **will never be persuaded**, trying to convince him that he must go to Troy? Or is the tone provocative?

- How important is it that Philoctetes no longer has his bow? Does this part of the exchange between Odysseus and Philoctetes seem consistent with Odysseus' character as represented elsewhere?

1028–9 So, my father begot me to be a slave Philoctetes uses the metaphor of slavery to express his lack of personal freedom.

1037 Hold him. Prevent him from moving In another sequence of dramatic moves Philoctetes attempts (or threatens) suicide and Odysseus has him tied up, displaying his complete physical control: Philoctetes is not free even to end his own life.

- In a production, would it be more dramatically effective for this order to be carried out by guards arriving with Odysseus or by members of the Chorus? What difference might it make?

1038 My hands! Philoctetes again addresses a part of his body directly, perhaps while his hands are actually being bound (see note on Language, page 70).

Agon

An *agon* is a debate or argument which includes a pair of opposing speeches. It was a common feature of Greek tragedy (for example, between Jason and Medea in Euripides' *Medea* or Teucer, firstly with Menelaus and secondly with Agamemnon in Sophocles' *Ajax*).

a) Philoctetes' speech (1038–78)

Philoctetes had already pieced together much of what had happened by 1008–9. Here he seems to have developed a fuller understanding of Neoptolemus' position.

- What has Philoctetes been told during the course of the play about the prophecy? (See note on The prophecy, page 44.)

1052 friendless, alone, outlawed Philoctetes equates his state of isolation, with no friend (*a-philos*) and no *polis* (*a-polis*), to a living death. (See page 22, Aristotle's definition of man.)

PHILOCTETES Hateful man! What lies you invent! In using the
gods to shield yourself, you make them liars.

ODYSSEUS No. They represent truth. The journey must be made. 1025

PHILOCTETES I refuse.

ODYSSEUS And I say you will go. You must obey.

PHILOCTETES Ah, wretched! So, my father begot me to be a
slave, without freedom.

ODYSSEUS No. He begot one who rivals the best of us. And it is 1030
with us that you must capture Troy and overthrow it by force.

PHILOCTETES Never, no matter what kind of suffering I have
to endure. Not as long as I have the sheer rocks of this land.

ODYSSEUS And what will you do?

PHILOCTETES Throw myself from the cliffs and dash this head 1035
against the rocks.

ODYSSEUS Hold him. Prevent him from moving.

PHILOCTETES My hands! What you suffer! How you long for
your beloved bowstring! Caught and bound by this man – with
his sick thoughts, his ruthless mind. 1040
See how you managed once again to creep up on me and
hunt me down! I didn't know this boy, so you used him to
screen yourself. But he is too good for you; he and I are well
suited. All he knew was how to do what he was told. And now
it is clear he's finding things hard – partly because he has 1045
made a mistake and partly because of the way I've suffered.
Your black soul watched him closely from the shadows and
instructed him carefully. Against his nature, against his will,
you taught him how to do wrong and be good at it. And now,
villain, you intend to tie me up and take me away from this 1050
shore – the spot where you stranded me, leaving me
friendless, alone, outlawed, to a living death.
A curse on you. This has been my constant prayer. But the
gods have granted me nothing to give pleasure. You are full of
the joys of life, while my existence is wretched and marked 1055

1058–9 you joined them only because you had to Philoctetes' sense of the injustice of the world, shared with Neoptolemus at 440–4, seems to be bitterly confirmed by his experience. He refers here to the traditional story that Odysseus had feigned madness in order to escape fighting at Troy by pretending to plough the barren sands on the shores of his homeland, Ithaca. He was outwitted by the Greeks, who placed his baby son Telemachus in front of the plough: Odysseus displayed his sanity by stopping to avoid the child (see Background to the story, page v).

1060–1 Seven ships I brought Sophocles' account tallies with that of Homer in 'The Catalogue of Ships', *Iliad ii* (see Background to the story, page v).

1068–9 Wasn't that your pretext for getting rid of me? See lines 6–9 (**We couldn't begin to make offerings or sacrifice in peace …**).

Philoctetes' curse
Philoctetes moves from cursing only Odysseus at 1053 to cursing **them all** (1076). Lines 1156–7 suggest that he is including Neoptolemus and his crew in this curse.

● Can you explain this in the light of his words at 1042–9?

b) Odysseus' speech (1081–94)
Odysseus' response is formal and insultingly curt.

● Consider Odysseus' statement at 1082–4. What does Odysseus appear to understand by the words **justice**, **honour** and **righteous**?

1087–8 We have no need of you See note on The prophecy, page 44.

1088 Teucer Son of Telamon and half-brother of Ajax, famed for his skills as an archer.

only by pain; surrounded by troubles, I am laughed at by you
and by the sons of Atreus, the two commanders whose bidding
you perform. And yet when you sailed with them, you joined
them only because you had to, because they tricked you. I
wanted to sail with them, pitiable fool that I am. Seven ships 1060
I brought, but they cast me out dishonoured. You claim they
were responsible; they say it was you. And why are you
leading me off now? Why are you taking me away? What
for? I am nothing. As far as you are concerned, I've been
long dead. How is it, god-detested man, that you no longer 1065
notice my lameness or the fact that I smell? How can you
perform sacrifices to the gods if I come on board? How can
you ever offer up a libation? Wasn't that your pretext for
getting rid of me? May your death be a painful one!
For the wrong you have done this body you will die – if the 1070
gods care at all about justice. And I know that they do: you
would never have made this expedition for a pitiable wretch
like me if some divine power weren't driving you on.
Land of my fathers, gods who watch on high, take
vengeance. Take vengeance, if you feel any pity for me. 1075
Take vengeance, in time, on them all. My life is pitiable, but
if I could see them dead, I could believe that I was rid of my
infection.

CHORUS Hard words from this hard stranger, Odysseus. His
troubles have not softened him. 1080

ODYSSEUS There is much I could say in response to his words,
if it were appropriate. As it is, I have just one thing to say: I
adapt to what circumstances require. When justice and honour
are critical, you could find no one more righteous than me.
The desire always to win comes naturally to me, but in your 1085
case I make an exception: I am willing to give in to you. Let
him go. Don't hold him. Let him stay here. We have no need
of you: since we have your weapons here. We have Teucer
with us who has the necessary skill. And then there's me.

1090–1 … handling one of these and at keeping my aim straight
A reminder of the skill shown by the Odysseus of Homer's *Odyssey xxi*
(419–23) as he shoots effortlessly through the twelve axe handle-rings
set up as a contest for the suitors of his wife.

1091–2 Enjoy your walks on Lemnos Odysseus seems to be
gratuitously offensive and heightens Philoctetes' sense of despair and
outrage.

1096 parade among the Greeks Philoctetes might be expected to
have understood from Odysseus' words the significance of the
prophecy even if he had not done so before. However, his thoughts
remain fixed on the image of Odysseus' triumph in the Greek camp
(see 605–7, 966–7) and the corresponding shame for him: to be
stripped of his weapons without even going through the formality of
death! In heroic warfare it was customary to strip a defeated enemy of
his armour after killing him.

1106 *He'll* claim I'm too soft-hearted Neoptolemus is referring to
Odysseus. He tells the Chorus to wait with Philoctetes, hoping that
they may be able to persuade him. As Neoptolemus finally breaks his
silence, he moves off with Odysseus and the bow. Both his attempt to
soften the pain for Philoctetes and his hope that Philoctetes might
change his mind seem feeble and half-hearted. This is the epitome of
the **coward's victory** spoken of at 90.

SECOND *COMMUS* (1111–1268)

(See note on First *commus*, page 62.) *Philoctetes withdraws again from
human intercourse, addressing his cave in a song of grief and self-pity.
His decision not to leave the island is clear. The departure of
Neoptolemus leaves the Chorus alone with Philoctetes. They remonstrate
forcefully with him.*

I believe I'm as good as you at handling one of these and at   1090
keeping my aim straight! What do we need you for? Enjoy
your walks on Lemnos. Let's be on our way. Your special
prize bow should soon win for me the honour that was to be
yours.

PHILOCTETES Ah, no! Misery! What am I going to do? Are you   1095
going to parade among the Greeks dressed up in my weapons?

ODYSSEUS Don't bother replying. I am leaving.

PHILOCTETES Son of Achilles! Am I not going to hear your
voice again? Is this how you leave?

ODYSSEUS You, move away. Don't look at him, whatever your   1100
noble feelings. I don't want you destroying our good fortune.

PHILOCTETES And am I going to be deserted by you, too,
friends? Won't you show me some pity?

CHORUS This boy is our captain. Whatever he says, we say the
same.   1105

NEOPTOLEMUS *He'll* claim I'm too soft-hearted. Never mind.
You wait here, if he wants you to, while the sailors get the
ship ready and we offer up our prayers to the gods. Perhaps in
the meantime he'll think more as we do. We'll go on ahead.
Come swiftly when we call you.   1110

PHILOCTETES   Cave of hollowed rock,
                    Now hot, now icy cold,
                     My wretched destiny
                     Never to leave you.
                You will be with me when I die.   1115
                        Ah, misery.

                     Chamber of grief,
                    So full of my sad pain,
                How will I live from day to day?

The Chorus

The Chorus were instructed by Neoptolemus to wait with Philoctetes, if he wanted them to, in the hope that he might change his mind. However, in the exchange that follows, Philoctetes seems hardly to hear them.

- To whom do you think Philoctetes is referring in lines 1145–8 and 1149–52? Is it clear?
- At what stage(s) in the second *commus* (1111–1268) does Philoctetes respond directly to the Chorus?
- Analyse the advice given by the Chorus to Philoctetes in 1127–35, 1153–8, 1176–82 and 1200–9. How fair are their comments and criticism?
- How independent a role does the Chorus seem to play in this *commus*?

Odysseus and Philoctetes. Silver cup from the 1st century BC.

What hope   1120
Has a useless wretch like me,
Of finding food?
Where would it come from?
Timorous birds, fly on above
Through the sharp breezes: 1125
I can catch you no more.

CHORUS   But it was you,
You who decided this course.
Your fate is heavy,
But not because of   1130
Some higher power.
When you had the chance
To make up your mind,
It was not the happier lot you chose,
But the worse.   1135

PHILOCTETES   Misery! Misery!
Broken by suffering
Never again will I be with others
But living in misery
Die here.   1140

Alas! Alas!
No more will I bring back food.
No arrows will fly from my bow
Gripped in my sure hand.

Deceptive words   1145
From a treacherous heart
Have caught me off guard
And stolen into me.

I wish I could see
The one who contrived this   1150
Enduring my portion of misery
For as long as I have.

1156 Keep your hateful, ill-fated curse for others See note on
Philoctetes' curse, page 76.

1157 our friendship
What claim to friendship do you think the Chorus are entitled to
make?

1160–1 He ... laughs at me For a hero, the laughter of an enemy is
unendurable: Ajax is driven to suicide and Medea to infanticide in
order to avoid it. Philoctetes' distress at this humiliation is evident
here and at 1056, but he is helpless to avoid it.

1164 Beloved bow Philoctetes addresses the bow in an extended
passage (see note on Language, page 70). The bow is made to seem
animate, like an absent friend or lover: he imagines it in another
man's hands, watching Odysseus as he sits on the shore.

1170 A wily master An allusion to *polu-mētis* ('of many wiles'), which
is Odysseus' stock epithet in the *Odyssey*. The word used here is *polu-
mēchanē* ('much-scheming').

Responsibility

1179 He was singled out from the mass The Chorus defend
Odysseus' behaviour by saying that he was acting under orders. This is
what Odysseus said of his actions at line 4. It also echoes the words of
Neoptolemus at 382–5 and 949–50, and, to some extent, of Philoctetes
himself at 1057–8 (see also 1061–2).

- How convincing do you find this defence?
- Is the fact that he acted **on behalf of his friends** significant?
- Can you think of any modern equivalents to this argument?
- Does it excuse Neoptolemus' behaviour?

CHORUS   It was destiny from the gods
                Not treachery from us
                    Which got you.   1155
        Keep your hateful, ill-fated curse for others,
            And don't reject our friendship.
                That matters to us.

PHILOCTETES   Ah, misery!
                He sits by the shore of the grey sea   1160
                    And laughs at me.
        Waving in his hand my means of survival
                Which no one touched till now.
                    Beloved bow,
                Wrenched from loving hands!   1165
            If you can feel, you must pity
                Heracles' poor companion
            Who will never use you again.
                You have changed hands:
                A wily master holds you now.   1170
        You see the shameful deceptions
            Of this spiteful, hateful man,
            The countless wrongs he has,
                In his shamelessness,
                Contrived against us.   1175

CHORUS   A man should say what he thinks is right,
                But once he's spoken,
        There should be an end to grudging, hurtful words.
            He was singled out from the mass
                And given his instructions.   1180
            He has performed a service
                On behalf of his friends.

1192 Time to get your own back now Philoctetes returns again and again to the ironies of his situation: the hunter becomes hunted; the eater becomes food (see also note on 277). He seems to revel in the details.

1196 What means have I to stay alive? Since Odysseus' orders to untie Philoctetes at 1086–7 and his departure, the option of suicide mentioned at 1035–6 has been open. However, what then was an exercise of freedom now represents a lack of choice: death is Philoctetes' only option. The Chorus insist that this is not the case (1206).

1201 If you feel any reverence for a stranger The Chorus now speak in general terms of themselves as 'strangers' or guest-friends (*xenoi*): their attempts to help have so far been ignored. Perhaps this is why they offer advice now as *xenoi* rather than *philoi*. (See note on line 399.)

Self-pity

- Is Philoctetes being melodramatic? Is his self-pity justified? What has made him decide to stay despite the horror of the life he predicts for himself?
- Do you think a director would want an audience to feel sympathy or alienation at this point in the play?

Philoctetes on Lemnos. Attic red figure lekythos (c. 430 BC).

PHILOCTETES
Winged birds of the air,
And all you bright-eyed creatures
Which these rocky uplands hold,   1185
Fly no more from your shelter in fear.
My hands no longer have their former power:
Without my arrows I am lost.
Run freely!
My lameness ensures   1190
You needn't fear me any longer.
Time to get your own back now,
To satisfy your appetites
On my discoloured flesh.
My death will come soon: 1195
What means have I to stay alive?
Can a man live on thin air
When he no longer has the power to take
What the life-giving earth offers him?

CHORUS
In the name of the gods,   1200
If you feel any reverence for a stranger,
Come to meet him:
The approach was made in all kindness.
But know this,
And know it well.   1205
It is in your power to escape this death,
Which is eating away at you pitifully,
Sharing your life, but unable to teach you
How to endure such suffering.

PHILOCTETES
Again, again, my ancient pain!   1210
Even you, the kindest
Of all who have come here,
dwell on it.

1223 Come on, let's go Neoptolemus instructed the Chorus to stay only if they were wanted. Their relief at leaving is evident.

1225 Don't go! As Philoctetes faces the prospect of being left alone again, he appeals to the Chorus to stay (1225, 1227, 1235). The Chorus respond with a question: **To do what?** There seems to be no solution: the Chorus cannot stay and Philoctetes makes it clear again – and in the strongest terms – that he will not leave (1242).

	Why have you destroyed me?	
	What have you done to me?	1215
CHORUS	What do you mean?	
PHILOCTETES	You hoped to take me to the land	
	I hate most – to Troy.	
CHORUS	It is for the best.	
PHILOCTETES	Leave me now. Go!	1220
CHORUS	I'm glad. Glad that's what you say.	
	It's what I've been wanting to do.	
	Come on, let's go. Let's go!	
	Back to our stations on board.	

PHILOCTETES	Don't go! I entreat you, by Zeus, god of prayers.	1225
CHORUS	Control yourself.	
PHILOCTETES	Strangers, wait! In the name of the gods.	
CHORUS	Why do you cry out?	
PHILOCTETES	Alas! Alas!	
	Misfortune! Misfortune!	1230
	I am ruined, wretched!	
	O my foot, my foot!	
	What will I do with you	
	In the wretched life that lies before us?	
	Strangers, come back, return to me again.	1235

CHORUS	To do what?	
	Have you changed your mind?	
PHILOCTETES	You shouldn't be angry	
	If raging pain makes a man distraught	
	and he cries out senselessly.	1240
CHORUS	Then come, poor wretch. Do as we ask.	
PHILOCTETES	Never! Never! That is final.	
	Not even if the fiery god of lightning,	
	Blazing in a thunderous flash	
	Should come at me.	1245

1253 A sword. Give me a sword, or an axe Philoctetes again threatens suicide (see also 1035–6, and the note on Death, page 60), but at 1264 he longs to see his homeland again alive. This fitful inconsistency is like his attitude towards Neoptolemus and his crew (see note on Philoctetes' curse, page 76).

1259 To search for my father At this moment of deepest self-pity Philoctetes' thoughts turn again to his father. He made a similar reference to Poeas at 478–81, another moment of dramatic intensity. There, Philoctetes expressed uncertainty as to whether his father was dead or alive, concluding that he must have died. Here, he has lost all hope.

1265 sacred streams The River Spercheius.

Review of the second *commus*
During the *commus* (1223–4), the Chorus prepare for their departure (*exodos*) which would normally mark the very end of the play. This turns out to be another false exit (see Another delay…, page 66). Much of Greek tragedy seems static, but Philoctetes' long lament in the second *commus* might seem particularly so. Consider the impact music and dance might have in performing this section of the play. The Chorus often serve a double function, both commenting on and being involved in the action (see Review of the first *stasimon*, page 54). Can these different functions be separated here?

EXODOS (1269–1543)
Exodos is the term both for the exit of the Chorus and for the final episode of the play.

The return of Odysseus
It is clear from lines 1326–7 that Philoctetes returns to his cave after line 1268.

The bracketed lines heralding the arrival of Odysseus in pursuit of Neoptolemus may not have been part of the original text. Their entry is certainly more dramatic without these lines!

o Consider different ways of staging this entry.

A mistake
Neoptolemus claims that in following the orders of the Greek army he has made a mistake (*hamartia*). This is significant for the debate which is to follow about the nature of right and wrong (see note on Justice, page 90).

To hell with Troy
And every man beneath her walls
Who joined in the cruelty
Of casting me out
With this foot.   1250
But, strangers, grant me one prayer.

CHORUS   What is it you want?
PHILOCTETES A sword. Give me a sword, or an axe,
                Any weapon you can find.
CHORUS   And what will you do with it?   1255
PHILOCTETES Sever my head from my limbs with this hand.
                My mind is set on death. Death.
CHORUS   Why?
PHILOCTETES   To search for my father.
CHORUS   And where is he?   1260
PHILOCTETES   In the land of the dead.
                He no longer sees the light of day.
                O my homeland, my fatherland,
                    How I long to look on you.
                    I left your sacred streams   1265
                – poor fool – and went to help
                    My enemies, the Greeks.
                    I am nothing now.

CHORUS   [I would have left you and returned to the ship long
    ago, but look! Odysseus is here and is coming towards us with   1270
    Achilles' son.]
ODYSSEUS Tell me why you've turned back? Where are you
    going in such a rush?
NEOPTOLEMUS I am going to undo a mistake I made earlier.
ODYSSEUS Your words alarm me. What mistake is this?   1275
NEOPTOLEMUS One I made in obedience to you and the whole
    army.

Justice

At 1303–13 Neoptolemus and Odysseus argue about justice. Various definitions of justice are offered in Book 1 of Plato's *Republic* and then shown by the philosopher Socrates to be inadequate:

a) Justice is returning what is due.

b) Justice is helping friends and harming enemies.

c) Justice is the interest of the stronger party (i.e. what those in authority determine).

- Consider the views that Odysseus has expressed during the course of the play (see 48–124, 1002–3, 1081–4). How close are his views to definition c)?

Neoptolemus has found an instance of justice that directly opposes 'the interest of the stronger party' (in this case, the interest of the Greek army).

- Is either definition a) or b) any more helpful in providing a definition? If not, what further element is required?

Stichomythia

The quick-fire, line-for-line exchanges between Odysseus and Neoptolemus create tension in this scene.

- What change is there in the balance of their relationship?
- How might this be shown on stage?

ODYSSEUS What have you done that you shouldn't have?

NEOPTOLEMUS I used shameful deception and trickery in catching him. 1280

ODYSSEUS Who do you mean? You're not intending some new move, are you?

NEOPTOLEMUS Nothing new. It concerns the son of Poeas.

ODYSSEUS What is it you are going to do? This is frightening me.

NEOPTOLEMUS I took this bow from him. I am going to 1285 return...

ODYSSEUS Zeus! What are you about to say? You're not thinking of *giving* it to him?

NEOPTOLEMUS I was wrong to take it. I have no right to keep it.

ODYSSEUS In god's name, are you saying this to provoke me? 1290

NEOPTOLEMUS If speaking the truth is provocation.

ODYSSEUS What do you mean, son of Achilles? What did you say?

NEOPTOLEMUS Do you want me to go over this again – and again? 1295

ODYSSEUS I didn't want to hear it the first time.

NEOPTOLEMUS Accept it, then, now you've heard all I have to say.

ODYSSEUS There is someone – someone who will stop you from doing this.

NEOPTOLEMUS What do you mean? Who is going to stop me?

ODYSSEUS Every man in Greece – myself included! 1300

NEOPTOLEMUS You may be wise yourself, but your words are not.

ODYSSEUS Nor are yours – and nor will your actions be.

NEOPTOLEMUS Perhaps not wise, but they are just – and that matters more than wisdom.

ODYSSEUS And how is it 'just' to give something back that you 1305 took under my direction?

NEOPTOLEMUS I made a shameful mistake. I am going to try to put it right.

ODYSSEUS And, in acting like this, aren't you afraid of the Greek army? 1310

1313 The original line is missing from the Greek text.

Exit Odysseus

The argument threatens to become violent, but an immediate conflict is avoided when Neoptolemus faces Odysseus out (see note on The young teaching the old, page 96).

- Why does Odysseus give way and leave Neoptolemus with the bow? Is he gracious or resentful? How threatening a figure does he present?
- Consider different ways in which an actor playing the role might move off-stage.

Neoptolemus and Philoctetes: rebuilding trust

Neoptolemus calls Philoctetes out of his cave. Philoctetes is full of suspicion and pessimism. This meeting contrasts with the openness and optimism of their first meeting at 243: the sweet sounds of Greek (254) have become **noise** and **shouting** (1328).

Language

We have seen how Aristotle viewed language as a defining characteristic of man and as the means by which values and ideals can be communicated and developed (see note on Language, page 32). For Philoctetes, language has been perverted by Neoptolemus and words have become **pointless** (1341 and 1346). 'Speech' has become mere 'voice', like that of an animal. Neoptolemus' former 'sincerity' only makes the job of persuading Philoctetes to listen to him even harder. (See also lines 1443 and 1457.)

1335 Isn't it possible to alter one's opinion? The audience have seen Neoptolemus reject Odysseus and his mission, but Philoctetes was not present to witness that encounter. Why should Philoctetes believe Neoptolemus now rather than suspect that he is there to put into effect earlier threats to remove him by force (1014) or to persuade him (573–4, 589)?

NEOPTOLEMUS With justice on my side, your army doesn't frighten me.

ODYSSEUS Perhaps there are some things a man should fear.

NEOPTOLEMUS Not even your hand can command my obedience. 1315

ODYSSEUS Then our war is not with the Trojans, but with you.

NEOPTOLEMUS So be it.

ODYSSEUS You see my hand, how lightly it rests on the hilt.

NEOPTOLEMUS And you see that I do the same. No more hesitation. 1320

ODYSSEUS I'll let you go, but I will be reporting these words to the entire army. They will be the ones who take vengeance on you.

NEOPTOLEMUS That's sensible. You may keep clear of trouble if you show as much good sense in the future. 1325
You, Philoctetes, son of Poeas, come out here. Leave your rocky cave.

PHILOCTETES What's this noise, this shouting outside my cave again? Why are you calling me out? What do you want, strangers? Ah, no. Bad news. Are you here to add to my 1330 misfortunes? To bring me further suffering?

NEOPTOLEMUS Take courage. Listen to what I have come to say.

PHILOCTETES I am full of fear. I trusted what you said before, and suffered because of your fine words.

NEOPTOLEMUS Isn't it possible to alter one's opinion? 1335

PHILOCTETES This is how you spoke to me when you stole my bow. You inspire trust, but secretly betray it.

NEOPTOLEMUS Not any more! I want to hear whether your decision is to remain here resolutely, or to sail with us.

PHILOCTETES Stop. Don't say any more. Anything you say 1340 will be pointless.

NEOPTOLEMUS That's your decision?

PHILOCTETES Yes: more certain than *words* of mine can express.

1348 deprived me of my means of living See note on 957–8.

Word and action

At 93–4 Odysseus said **it is always what people say rather than what they do that makes the difference**: this is not true in this case. Neoptolemus' words fail to convince Philoctetes, but the simple action of returning the bow has far greater power.

- Consider the extent to which words have been used to deceive or confuse in the play as a whole.

Staging Odysseus' return: high drama or melodrama?

Just as Neoptolemus and Philoctetes are on the point of re-establishing trust, Odysseus suddenly reappears. The parallels with his appearance at 1002 are notable: in each case Neoptolemus is handing the bow to Philoctetes when Philoctetes hears his enemy's voice (1004–5, 1364–5). The outcome of this final, brief meeting is different: Philoctetes takes the bow from Neoptolemus and the encounter feared by Odysseus in the Prologue is realised.

- How could a director emphasise the parallels and differences between the action at 1002 and here (1364) (see An alternative appeal, page 34)?
- At what point and how do you imagine Philoctetes gaining control of the bow? (Some lines might suggest that Philoctetes is capable of sudden movement – see 459–60, 1035–7 and 1225.) What part does Neoptolemus play in this?
- How close is Odysseus when he speaks? Is he alone or accompanied by more men than at 1270–1? At what point does he leave? How might he do so?

- Does this encounter add to or detract from the play as a whole?

The character of Odysseus

We saw in the note on lines 137–8 that Sophocles' Odysseus in *Philoctetes* incorporates most of the traditional Homeric characteristics (cunning, the support of Athene, etc.). However, Greek dramatists felt free to develop characters within these set parameters to suit their drama. Odysseus also appears in Sophocles' *Ajax*, but there he appears as a far more attractive and sympathetic character.

- How consistent a character is Odysseus in this play? (See Prologue and note on characterisation, page 8.)
- Compare Odysseus' behaviour here and at 1272–1323. Is Odysseus cowardly (1379)? Does he have any redeeming qualities?

NEOPTOLEMUS But I wanted to talk to you and convince you. If I'm speaking out of turn, I'll stop.

PHILOCTETES Anything you say is pointless. You will never meet with any warmth from me: you took my bow by trickery and deprived me of my means of living. And then you come here to give me advice! Your father was a fine man, but you I hate. Death take you all: the sons of Atreus first, then Laertes' son – and you.

NEOPTOLEMUS Hold your prayers. Take from my hand these weapons.

PHILOCTETES What did you say? Are we to be tricked a second time?

NEOPTOLEMUS I swear that is not so – by the sacred majesty of Zeus on high.

PHILOCTETES These are words I long to hear, if only you speak them truly!

NEOPTOLEMUS Action will reveal their truth. Stretch out your right hand and take possession of your weapons.

ODYSSEUS I forbid this, as the gods are my witnesses, on behalf of the sons of Atreus and the entire army.

PHILOCTETES Child, whose voice did I hear? It belongs to Odysseus, doesn't it?

ODYSSEUS Be sure of it. And here, before you, is the man who will take you to Troy's plain by force, whether Achilles' son likes it or not.

PHILOCTETES It will bring you no joy – not if this arrow flies straight!

NEOPTOLEMUS No! By the god, don't do it! Don't shoot!

PHILOCTETES In god's name, let go of my hand, my dear, dear child.

NEOPTOLEMUS I won't.

PHILOCTETES Ah, no! The man was my bitter enemy – why did you stop me killing him with an arrow?

1345

1350

1355

1360

1365

1370

1375

1377 Neither of us would win any honour from it Neoptolemus displays a wisdom and maturity that contrast both with his naïve questioning of Odysseus at 121–2 and with Philoctetes' petulant desire for revenge (see note on The young teaching the old, below).

1384 *Your* father was no Sisyphus See note on 411.

1385–6 and now the finest of the dead The audience was perhaps reminded of Homer's vision of Achilles when Odysseus meets him in the land of the dead (*Odyssey xi* (482–92)).

The young teaching the old

Earlier in the play both Odysseus and Philoctetes instructed the young Neoptolemus how to win a glorious reputation (see An alternative appeal, page 34). Now Neoptolemus seems to have become the teacher, lecturing firstly Odysseus on justice and wisdom (1303–1325) and then Philoctetes on the will of the gods and the path to glory (1388–1413).

That 'the young teaching the old' was seen by some people in fifth-century Athens as an inversion of the natural order of things is suggested by the comic treatment of sons trying to educate their recalcitrant fathers in Aristophanes' *Wasps* and *Clouds*. In Sophocles' *Antigone* the judgement of the ruler, Creon, is tactfully questioned by his son, Haemon, who is later shown to have greater understanding of the gods' will than his stubborn father. In *Philoctetes*, as in *Antigone*, Sophocles seems to be challenging the assumption that wisdom is the prerogative of age and authority.

1401–2 sons of Asclepius Asclepius is the god of healing. His sons, Machaon and Podalirius, feature in Homer's *Iliad*, and in later accounts both are individually credited with healing Philoctetes (see note on 1512). This is the first mention of a cure for Philoctetes' foot.

1403–4 you ... will be known as the one who sacked the citadel Neoptolemus offers Philoctetes the same *kleos* that drove him to accept Odysseus' mission at 125 (see note on *kleos*, page 20). He now seems to understand that this glory is to be shared (see also note on 1511).

NEOPTOLEMUS Neither of us would win any honour from it.

PHILOCTETES But we learn this much – that the leaders of the
army, those lying heralds of Greece, are cowards when it
comes to a fight, for all their bold talk! 1380

NEOPTOLEMUS There. You have the bow, and that means
you've no grounds for being angry with me or blaming me.

PHILOCTETES Agreed. You have shown your true nature, child,
the one you were born with. *Your* father was no Sisyphus, but
Achilles, the finest of men while he was alive, and now the 1385
finest of the dead.

NEOPTOLEMUS It gives me pleasure to hear you speak well of
my father – and of myself. Listen to what I ask of you. Men
must bear the fortune the gods give them. People who cling to
self-inflicted injuries, like you, have no right to anyone's 1390
sympathy or pity. You have turned wild: you accept no
advice, and, even when someone tries to offer a friendly word
of warning, you are full of hate and assume he is your bitter
enemy. I am nevertheless going to speak out. I call on Zeus,
god of oaths. Understand this, inscribe it in your brain. You 1395
are sick, and the source of your suffering is divine – you went
near the guardian of Chryse, a snake who guards the roofless
enclosure, watching over it from its hiding place. You will
never find rest from this sickening affliction as long as the
sun continues to rise and set where it does, unless you go of 1400
your own free will to the plain of Troy, meet with the sons of
Asclepius who are with us there, and find relief from this
disease; you, together with these weapons and my help,
will be known as the one who sacked the citadel.

1413 loud-lamented The compound adjective (*polu-stonon*) has a Homeric ring (see note on 1170). There are other examples of this, for example, Lemnos is described as *surrounded by sea* (lines 1–2 and 1534).

The prophecy

The audience is entitled to feel some confusion about the terms of the prophecy! Odysseus first informed Neoptolemus of the need for Philoctetes' bow at 113; no mention was made of Philoctetes himself until the Merchant's speech (588) and then nothing was said of a cure. The Chorus advised Neoptolemus to leave with the bow while Philoctetes slept, and Odysseus' words at 1087–8 maintain that the bow alone is required. On the other hand, although Neoptolemus' 'prophetic words' (see page 62), stating that both the man *and* the bow are required, are developed in this speech, the basis of his assurance in 1400–4, as at 855–9, is far from clear!

- If Neoptolemus *had* heard Helenus' prophecy, how might we explain Neoptolemus' question at 114–15?

The audience's confusion perhaps makes it easier for us to understand Philoctetes' uncertainty: at times, he has sensed divine powers at work (1073), but why should he believe the conflicting accounts of the prophecy he has heard from men he cannot trust?

- How persuasive and well directed are Neoptolemus' words? How do you anticipate Philoctetes will respond?

I will tell you how I know that this is so: we took a prisoner at   1405
Troy, a skilled prophet called Helenus, and he said clearly that
these things must be. That is not all: this summer Troy must
be completely overthrown. He is prepared to die if his words
are false.

Now that you know, come along willingly. The prize will be   1410
a fair one! To be singled out as the champion of Greece! To
find hands that can heal you and to win the ultimate glory for
the loud-lamented capture of Troy!

PHILOCTETES Hateful life! Why keep me alive any longer? Let
me sink into the house of Death. Oh, what can I do? How can   1415
I not believe what he says? His advice was offered in kindness.
Should I give in, then? But if I do, how could I appear in
public, cursed as I am by fate? Who would speak to me? O,
vaults of heaven, who have witnessed all that has happened to
me, how could you bear to see me in the company of the   1420
sons of Atreus, the very men who destroyed me?

Philoctetes' response

In this *agon* (see note on page 74), Philoctetes' reaction is clear from his first words. At first he does not respond directly to Neoptolemus, but addresses **life** (1414) and later the sky (1419) – part of his introverted world (see note on Language, page 70). He makes no reference to the prophecies and his words are driven by *his* perception of events. Odysseus and the sons of Atreus are his sworn enemies; he is adamant in his refusal to help them and fearful of their intentions. Moreover, he believes Neoptolemus' story of how he was denied his father's arms (see note on Audience uncertainty: the arms of Achilles, page 26).

kakos

In Philoctetes' speech (1414–35) the word *kakos* appears six times. It is difficult to translate with a single word. Philoctetes' argument is that the leaders at Troy are incurably *kakoi* ('bad/evil/base/cowardly/worthless') and deserve to come to a bad (*kakon*) end. Neoptolemus should not help them lest he become *kakos* like them. Neoptolemus' words at 382–5 were very similar: the words 'vicious', 'vile' and 'corrupt' are all possible translations of *kakos*.

1434 from me and from my father In a more optimistic mood than at 1259–61, Philoctetes now speaks of Poeas as though he were alive.

- Is Philoctetes' inconsistency over this matter plausible?
- Are there other respects in which Philoctetes is inconsistent?

The character of Philoctetes

- Is Philoctetes' response in 1414–35 purely selfish? Is he so stubborn that it is difficult for the audience to sympathise with him?
- Why should Philoctetes trust Neoptolemus?

Could you see me with Laertes' deadly son? It's not the
pain of what's past that eats away at me; it is the prospect of
what I can anticipate suffering at their hands in the future. A
mind that has given birth to evil, nurtures evil ever after. This   1425
is what makes me surprised at your behaviour: you, who
should never have gone to Troy yourself, should be stopping
me from going there! They insulted you, stripped you of your
father's prizes of honour. These are the men on whose side
you are intending to fight – and you're making me do   1430
the same. Don't, child! Do what you swore to me you'd do: take
me home. And as for yourself, stay on Scyros and let base
men die as they deserve! In this way you will earn twice the
gratitude, from me and from my father. And by refusing to
help them, you will not seem base yourself.   1435

NEOPTOLEMUS What you say is fair, but I still want you to
trust the gods and believe what I've said. Leave this land and
come away with someone who cares for you.

PHILOCTETES To the plain of Troy and my enemy, Atreus'
son, with my foot afflicted like this?   1440

NEOPTOLEMUS To those who will stop your pain, heal your
festering foot and save you from this sickness.

PHILOCTETES O, teller of clever tales, what do you really mean?

NEOPTOLEMUS I am thinking of what will be best for you and
me in the end.   1445

1446 And in saying this ... The dialogue between Neoptolemus and Philoctetes strongly recalls the dialogue between Odysseus and Neoptolemus in the Prologue (lines 106–12).

● Compare the two situations.

1468–9 When you took my right hand, you vowed you would take me home

● Did he? (See 820–1; also 963–4 and 1431–2.)

A surprise twist?

Just when the situation seems hopeless, Philoctetes again pleads with Neoptolemus to take him back to Greece as he swore he would (see also 1431–2). This time Neoptolemus agrees.

● Is his decision surprising?

kleos sacrificed

At line 125 it was the prospect of *kleos* (see note on page 20) that led Neoptolemus to agree to support Odysseus. At 1472 he surrenders that prospect. His father Achilles makes a similar decision in answer to the embassy in *Iliad ix*, when he is offered fine gifts as compensation from Agamemnon for a slight to his honour and is asked to rejoin the fighting at Troy. His divine mother, Thetis, informs him that he has a choice between a long life at home without glory and a brief life bringing everlasting fame. Achilles' decision to go home and reject the life which brings *kleos* shocks his comrades.

● Compare the circumstances and implications of Neoptolemus' and Achilles' decision to renounce *kleos*.
● Why do you think Neoptolemus makes the decision he does?
● How reassuring are Philoctetes' responses to the worries expressed by Neoptolemus in lines 1476–83?

The character of Neoptolemus

● Which of the following words best suit Neoptolemus' character: *weak, kind, selfish, noble, naïve, brave, arrogant, selfless, ambitious, frank*?
● To what extent and how do you feel that Neoptolemus' character develops over the course of the play?

PHILOCTETES And in saying this, don't you feel any shame before the gods?

NEOPTOLEMUS Why should someone feel shame in helping a friend?

PHILOCTETES By that do you mean helping the sons of Atreus, or helping me?   1450

NEOPTOLEMUS I am your friend. My words show this.

PHILOCTETES How can that be when you want to deliver me up to the enemy?

NEOPTOLEMUS My friend, you are in trouble – learn some humility.   1455

PHILOCTETES You will destroy me with your words, I *know* you!

NEOPTOLEMUS I will not. You don't understand.

PHILOCTETES Don't I? I know it was the sons of Atreus who cast me out.   1460

NEOPTOLEMUS They cast you out, but see if they don't prove your salvation.

PHILOCTETES Never – if that means choosing to see Troy again.

NEOPTOLEMUS What can I do if nothing I say to you can convince you? It's time for me to stop talking and for you to   1465 get on with your life, the life you live now, a life without redemption.

PHILOCTETES Leave me to suffer what I must suffer. When you took my right hand, you vowed you would take me home. Do that for me, child. And don't delay or mention Troy any   1470 more. I've had more than enough of chattering talk.

NEOPTOLEMUS If that is what you want, let us go.

PHILOCTETES Spoken with true nobility.

NEOPTOLEMUS Step carefully.

PHILOCTETES As far as my strength allows.   1475

NEOPTOLEMUS How will I escape the reproaches of the Greeks?

PHILOCTETES Don't let it concern you.

NEOPTOLEMUS But what if they come to ravage my country?

PHILOCTETES I will be there.

Modern adaptations

The poet Seamus Heaney wrote a version of *Philoctetes* in 1990 titled *The Cure at Troy*. Although keeping close to the original in the rest of his version, he inserts an additional passage for the Chorus after line 1484 in which he alludes to contemporary Irish politics:

Human beings suffer,
They torture one another,
They get hurt and get hard.
No poem or play or song
Can fully right a wrong
Inflicted and endured.

The innocent in gaols
Beat on their bars together.
A hunger-striker's father
Stands in the graveyard dumb.
The police widow in veils
Faints at the funeral home.

History says, 'Don't hope
On this side of the grave'.
But then, once in a lifetime
The longed-for tidal wave
Of justice can rise up,
And hope and history rhyme.

So hope for a great sea-change
On the far side of revenge.
Believe that a further shore
Is reachable from here.
Believe in miracles
And cures and healing wells.

Call miracle self-healing:
The utter self-revealing
Double-take of feeling.
If there's fire on the mountain
Or lightning and storm
And a god speaks from the sky

That means someone is hearing
The outcry and the birth-cry
Of new life at its term.

- How do Heaney's words relate to Neoptolemus' decision to help Philoctetes?
- Why do you think Heaney chose this point for these additional lines? (You may need to read to the end of the play to answer this.)
- Do you feel that the issues involved in *Philoctetes* can be related convincingly to the Troubles in Northern Ireland? Can you think of other settings that might 'work' in production?

Philoctetes asleep in Heaney's 'Cure at Troy', Jean Cocteau Repertory production, New York, 1997.

DEUS EX MACHINA (1485–1543)

This is the only surviving play by Sophocles in which a god is brought on at the end of the play to resolve the action of the drama (although in *Ajax*, the goddess Athene appears at the start of the play). The ancient Greek theatre had a device for swinging immortals high into view, probably onto the roof of the *skēnē* (see Introduction to the Greek Theatre, page 114). This type of ending was frequently used in plays by other authors. In *The Art of Poetry* (chapter 15) Aristotle states:

> The unravelling of the plot should arise from the circumstances of the plot itself .... The *deus ex machina* should be used only for matters outside the play proper, either for things that happened before it and cannot be known by the human characters, or for things that are yet to come and require to be told prophetically – for we allow to the gods the power to see all things.'

(Trans. Dorsch)

- Do you think Sophocles' use of the *deus ex machina* works well in this play? Does it fulfil the requirements of Aristotle's *The Art of Poetry*?
- How might the sudden appearance of the god be staged in a modern production?

Heracles

Heracles was the mortal son of Zeus and Alcmene. Hera, Zeus' wife, tricked her husband into enslaving Heracles at birth to Eurystheus (*Iliad xix*), and Heracles was forced to perform a series of heroic labours (killing the Nemean Lion, Lernaean Hydra, etc.). On his death he was rewarded with divinity.

Heracles is mentioned frequently in the play because of his special relationship with Philoctetes, who lit his funeral pyre and in return received Heracles' bow (see index for references to Heracles). Philoctetes speaks of the service he performed for Heracles as **an act of kindness** (649) for which he has been rewarded only with misery. Heracles teaches him here that the rewards for his service are yet to come: cure from his sickness, the glory of sacking Troy, and a happy homecoming. Heracles makes no mention of the tradition that Philoctetes later leaves Greece and founds various cities in southern Italy.

1501 Paris, the originator of these troubles It was Paris' abduction of Helen, wife of Menelaus, that initiated the Trojan War. Philoctetes kills Paris in a duel.

1504–5 Oeta ... Poeas At last Philoctetes' doubts about whether his father is still alive are put to rest: he will return to Oeta, his homeland and the place where he first met Heracles.

NEOPTOLEMUS And what help can you give?   1480
PHILOCTETES Using the arrows of Heracles…
NEOPTOLEMUS But how?
PHILOCTETES …I will prevent their approach.
NEOPTOLEMUS Come, kiss this land farewell.

HERACLES   Not yet. Not until you hear   1485
                 What I have to say, child of Poeas.
             Acknowledge that it is the voice of Heracles
                You hear, and him you see before you.
                It is for your sake that I have come,
                   Leaving my seat in heaven,   1490
                  To proclaim Zeus' plans for you
             And to prevent the journey on which you embark.
                        Heed my words.

First, I will tell you of my own fortune: I endured much,
passed through a sequence of labours, and now I have attained   1495
divine glory, as you can see. Know that a like experience
awaits you: in exchange for your labours, a life of fame.
Go with this man to the citadel of Troy; and first find
respite from your grievous disease. For your valour, you will
be judged the army's champion. With these arrows of mine   1500
you will deprive Paris, the originator of these troubles, of life.
When you have sacked Troy you will send spoils to your
halls, taking first choice of the finest from all the army,
taking them to the plains of Oeta, your homeland, and to
your father, Poeas. And of the spoils that you receive from   1505
the army, take a dedicatory portion in thanks for my bow to
my pyre.
The same words apply to you, child of Achilles: without this
man you do not have the strength to capture the plain of
Troy, nor does he without you.   1510

1511 Like a pair of lions working together This striking simile dignifies both Neoptolemus and Philoctetes, but focuses in particular upon the nature of their relationship: one of mutual support and common purpose. Such animal similes are common in the *Iliad*.

1512 Asclepius The god of healing himself rather than his sons (see note on 1401–2) is to cure Philoctetes.

1513–14 Troy, which must fall a second time to my bow Heracles had taken part in an earlier expedition which had sacked Troy (see Background to the story, page v).

Neoptolemus: another tradition
The final words of Heracles' speech are addressed to Neoptolemus and are appropriate to the themes in this play, in particular the true nature of nobility and the general principle that man's understanding of the world and the workings of the gods is limited. But here it may have further resonances. Neoptolemus (or Pyrrhus – see note on line 55) appears elsewhere in art and literature in a very different light, perhaps most famously and influentially in Virgil's *Aeneid ii* where, far from showing reverence to the gods at the sack of Troy, he murders King Priam at an altar in view of Hecuba, his wife. This is the tradition that Shakespeare follows when the First Player recites to Hamlet the vile part played by Neoptolemus (whom he describes as 'hellish Pyrrhus') in the sack of Troy, in particular his cruel murder of the aged King Priam (Act II sc. ii).

A tragic ending?
The final departure, anticipated so many times during the course of the play (see Another delay…, page 66), brings the action to its end. The play opened with the arrival of the Greeks on **Lemnos, surrounded by sea** and closes with their departure, mission accomplished. This 'happy ending' does not conform with most people's expectations of what a 'tragedy' should be, but by no means all Greek tragedies end with physical mutilation, mental trauma or death. Most, however, explore serious questions about man's role in the world: questions of right and wrong; of justice and injustice; of man's interdependence; of his capacity to inflict and suffer evil; of the power of language.

- What other themes have been explored in the course of this play?
- How satisfactory do you consider this ending? How different a play would it have been if it had closed at 1484?

Like a pair of lions working together, keep guard – you over him and he over you. I will send Asclepius – who will be the one to heal your sickness – to Troy, which must fall a second time to my bow. But mark this: when you sack the land, show reverence to the gods. All other things take second place in the 1515 mind of our father, Zeus. Holy reverence outlasts man, neither in life nor in death can it be destroyed.

PHILOCTETES The voice I have longed for is here, appearing long after time. I shall not disobey your words.

NEOPTOLEMUS Nor I. 1520

HERACLES Do not be slow to act now. This is the moment, the wind is in your favour, urging you on.

PHILOCTETES Come, then.
And as I go, I will cry out to this land.

Farewell, watchful shelter, 1525
nymphs of the water meadows,
deep thunder of the crashing waves.
Often I have sheltered in a corner here,
my head wet from the lashings of the south wind.
Many times Mount Hermaeon has answered my cries 1530
with a sigh, when I have been caught by a storm.
I am leaving you now, streams and waters of Lycion,
Leaving now, though I never expected it.

Farewell, plain of Lemnos, surrounded by sea.
Send me on my voyage with a fair wind, 1535
Giving no cause for regret,
Guided by the power of Fate,
The advice of friends,
And the all-powerful god,
Who has brought these things to pass. 1540

CHORUS Let us all depart together
When we have prayed to the sea-nymphs
To bring us a safe journey home.

Synopsis of the play

PROLOGUE (1–138)

In the tenth year of the war against Troy, a Greek expedition arrives on the island of Lemnos. Neoptolemus, the young son of Achilles, and Odysseus are in command. Ten years earlier, on the same shore, Odysseus had deposited Philoctetes, who was suffering from an infected snakebite. The Greek commanders, who had found his cries of pain and the smell from his wound intolerable, had ordered this.

Neoptolemus and his men search the shore and find pathetic traces of Philoctetes' lonely existence, but not the man himself. A look-out is posted to watch out for Philoctetes' return: Odysseus fears his hatred and the power of the bow of Heracles.

Odysseus explains to Neoptolemus that Philoctetes must be tricked into returning to Troy: a prophecy has revealed that only with the bow of Heracles, which Philoctetes has in his possession, can Troy be taken. Neoptolemus, already aware of a prophecy affecting himself – that Achilles' son would sack Troy – realises that his own fame is at stake and agrees to help, but he is shocked by Odysseus' methods.

Once Odysseus is sure that Neoptolemus understands the plan, he returns to the safety of the ship, but arranges to send the look-out back, disguised as a merchant, if Neoptolemus seems to him to be taking too long.

PARODOS (139–242)

The Chorus, consisting of members of the crew, are already well informed, but question Neoptolemus about the mission. They express pity for Philoctetes' suffering, and apprehension when they hear his cries.

FIRST EPISODE (243–657)

Part 1 (243–387)

Philoctetes greets the strangers warmly, delighted to learn that they are fellow Greeks and that Neoptolemus is the son of his friend, Achilles. When Neoptolemus pretends not to know who he is, Philoctetes speaks of his suffering at the hands of Odysseus and the Greek commanders. Neoptolemus replies with his own story, rehearsed with Odysseus, of how the same commanders refused to give him his father's weapons.

FIRST CHORAL INTERLUDE (388–98)

The Chorus reinforce Neoptolemus' story.

Part 2 (399–487)

Philoctetes is shocked but not surprised by what Neoptolemus reveals. Their grievances seem to unite them, as do their sympathies. When Neoptolemus relates what he knows of those who have died at Troy, they agree that the world is unjust: good men suffer and die but the wicked flourish. When Neoptolemus then makes a move to depart, Philoctetes begs him to take him home to Greece.

SECOND CHORAL INTERLUDE (488–96)

The Chorus urge Neoptolemus to take Philoctetes on board.

Part 3 (497–657)

Neoptolemus agrees, but is deliberately vague about their destination. Philoctetes' delight in believing he is at last going home is interrupted by the arrival of two men, one of whom is the 'merchant' Odysseus said he would send.

The Merchant describes the capture by Odysseus of the Trojan seer, Helenus, and speaks of his prophecies. He tells of two separate plots against Neoptolemus and Philoctetes: Phoenix and the sons of Theseus have set out after Neoptolemus; and Odysseus, together with Diomedes, is looking for Philoctetes. Philoctetes expresses his absolute refusal to go to Troy – particularly not with Odysseus – and is more convinced than ever that he and Neoptolemus are fellow victims. As they again prepare to leave the island, Philoctetes allows Neoptolemus to hold his bow.

FIRST *STASIMON* (658–728)

While Neoptolemus and Philoctetes pay a last visit to the cave, the Chorus reflect upon Philoctetes' suffering and isolation. They contrast Philoctetes' unmerited fate with the just punishment of Ixion.

SECOND EPISODE (729–838)

Philoctetes and Neoptolemus emerge from the cave, but Philoctetes begins to suffer violent spasms of pain and they are forced to halt. Philoctetes entrusts his bow to Neoptolemus and beseeches him not to leave. Neoptolemus offers his hand as a sign of trust. Philoctetes' fit of pain worsens, and then he sleeps.

FIRST *COMMUS* (839–83)

The *commus* takes the place of the second *stasimon*. The Chorus sing to Sleep and recommend that Neoptolemus take advantage of the opportunity to escape with the bow. Neoptolemus speaks prophetically, indicating that without Philoctetes himself, the mission will fail.

THIRD EPISODE (884–1110)

Philoctetes wakes, but their passage to the ship is again halted. Neoptolemus, filled with shame at his part in the deception, confesses that he is to take Philoctetes to Troy. Philoctetes feels utterly betrayed and is furious. He pleads with Neoptolemus to return the bow, but at the critical moment Odysseus appears: he is in control as long as Philoctetes is unarmed. Odysseus threatens to take him to Troy by force, and prevents Philoctetes from trying to kill himself. Philoctetes refuses to go and cries out for vengeance. Odysseus suddenly releases him, claiming that it is only the bow he needs. As they leave, Philoctetes makes a final appeal to Neoptolemus who instructs his crew to stay and try to win Philoctetes round.

SECOND *COMMUS* (1111–1268)

This takes the place of the third *stasimon*. Philoctetes sings a song of self-pity, at first ignoring the Chorus, who urge him to seek a cure for his suffering and are critical of his refusal to cooperate. He appeals to them for sympathy but refuses to go to Troy, seeking death in preference.

EXODOS (1269–1543)

Philoctetes goes in misery back into his cave and Neoptolemus suddenly returns, pursued by Odysseus. He is determined to return the bow and openly disobeys Odysseus, who leaves when his threats are treated with contempt.

Philoctetes emerges from his cave, but views Neoptolemus with distrust. Unable to persuade Philoctetes of his integrity using words, Neoptolemus gives him back the bow. As Neoptolemus passes the bow, Odysseus springs out and tries to stop him, but it is too late. Armed again, Philoctetes tries to shoot his old enemy, but is prevented from doing so by Neoptolemus' timely intervention. Even with the bow restored, Philoctetes still does not trust Neoptolemus enough to go with him to Troy, and asks to be taken home to Greece instead. Neoptolemus agrees.

DEUS EX MACHINA (1485–1543)

Their departure is delayed once again by the appearance of Heracles. Philoctetes recognises his voice and is at last convinced by his divine words that glory and a cure for his wound lie at Troy, fighting side by side with Neoptolemus. The play ends as the expedition departs.

Pronunciation of names

To attempt an authentic pronunciation of classical Greek names presents great difficulties. It is perhaps easiest to accept the conventional anglicised versions of the familiar names (e.g. Achilles, Zeus). The key below offers help with all the names in the play, which will give a reasonable overall consistency. Note that the stress occurs on the italicised syllable.

> **KEY**
>
> ay – as in 'hay'   ch – as in Scottish 'loch'
> ē – as in 'hair'   ī – as in 'die'
> ō – long 'o', as in 'go'

Achaeans	A-*chee*-ans	Malis	*May*-lis
Achilles	A-*chil*-lees	Menelaus	Me-ne-*lay*-us
Agamemnon	A-ga-*mem*-nōn	Mycenae	My-*see*-nee
Ajax	*Ay*-jax	Neoptolemus	Ne-op-*to*-le-mus
Antilochus	An-*ti*-lo-chus	Nestor	*Nes*-tōr
Asclepius	As-*klee*-pi-us	Odysseus	O-*dis*-se-us
Athene	A-*thee*-nee	Oeta	*Oi*-ta
Atreidae	A-*tre*-i-dī	Patroclus	*Pat*-rok-lus
Atreus	*Ay*-tre-us	Peleus	*Pee*-le-us
Calchas	*Kal*-chas	Peparethos	Pe-*pa*-rē-thos
Cephallenia	Kefal-*lee*-nia	Philoctetes	Fi-lok-*tee*-tees
Chalcodon	Chal-*kō*-dōn	Phoenix	*Fee*-nix
Chryse	*Chrī*-see	Poeas	*Poi*-as
Cronus	*Kro*-nus	Priam	*Prī*-am
Diomedes	Dī-o-*mee*-dees	Pylos	*Pī*-los
Euboea	Yu-*bee*-a	Scyros	*Skī*-ros
Hades	*Hay*-dees	Sigeum	*Si*-ge-um
Helenus	*He*-le-nus	Sisyphus	*Si*-si-fus
Hephaestus	He-*fīs*-tus	Spercheius	Sper-*chay*-us
Heracles	*Hē*-rak-les	Teucer	*Tyoo*-ser
Hermes	*Her*-mees	Thersites	Ther-*sī*-tees
Ixion	*Ik*-si-ōn	Theseus	*Thee*-se-us
Laertes	Lay-*er*-tees	Tydeus	*Ti*-de-us
Lemnos	*Lem*-nos	Zeus	Zyoos
Lycomedes	Li-ko-*mē*-dees		

Introduction to the Greek Theatre

Theātron, the Greek word that gave us 'theatre' in English, meant both 'viewing place' and the assembled viewers. These ancient viewers (*theātai*) were in some ways very different from their modern counterparts. For a start, they were participants in a religious festival, and they went to watch plays only on certain days in the year, when shows were put on in honour of Dionysus. At Athens, where drama developed many of its most significant traditions, the main Dionysus festival, held in the spring, was one of the most important events in the city's calendar, attracting large numbers of citizens and visitors from elsewhere in the Greek world. It is not known for certain whether women attended; if any did, they were more likely to be visitors than the wives of Athenian citizens.

The festival was also a great sporting occasion. Performances designed to win the god's favour needed spectators to witness and share in the event, just as the athletic contests did at Olympia or Delphi, and one of the ways in which the spectators got involved was through competition. What they saw were three sets of three tragedies plus a satyr play, five separate comedies and as many as twenty song-and-dance performances called dithyrambs, put on in honour of Dionysus by choruses representing the different 'tribes' into which the citizen body was divided. There was a contest for each different event, with the dithyramb choruses divided into men's and boys' competitions, and a panel of judges determined the winners. The judges were appointed to act on behalf of the city; no doubt they took some notice of the way the audience responded on each occasion. Attendance at these events was on a large scale: we should be thinking of football crowds rather than typical theatre audiences in the modern world.

Like football matches, dramatic festivals were open-air occasions, and the performances were put on in daylight rather than with stage lighting in a darkened auditorium. The ideal performance space in these circumstances was a hollow hillside to seat spectators, with a flat area at the bottom (*orchēstra*) in which the chorusmen could spread out for their dancing and singing and which could be closed off by a stage-building (*skēnē*) acting simultaneously as backdrop, changing room and sounding board. Effective acoustics and good sight-lines were achieved by the kind of design represented in Fig. A on page 115, the theatre of Dionysus at Athens. The famous stone theatre at Epidaurus (Fig. B), built about 330 BC, and often taken as typical, has a circular *orchēstra*, but in the fifth century it was normal practice for

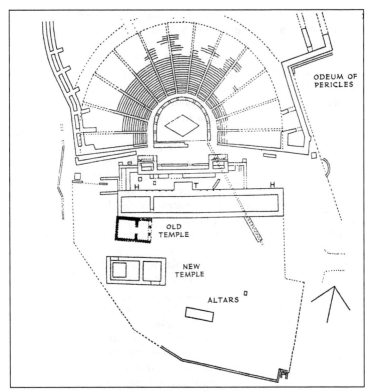

Fig. A. The theatre of Dionysus at Athens.

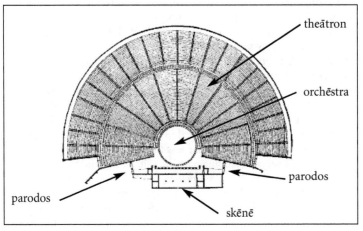

Fig. B. The theatre at Epidaurus (fourth century BC).

theatres to have a low wooden stage in front of the *skēnē*, for use by the actors, who also interacted with the chorus in the *orchēstra*.

Song and dance by choruses and the accompanying music of the piper were integral to all these types of performance and not just to the dithyramb. In tragedy there were 12 (later 15) chorusmen, in comedy 24, and in dithyramb 50; plays were often named after their chorus: Aeschylus' *Persians*, Euripides' *Bacchae*, Aristophanes' *Birds* are familiar examples. The rhythmic movements, groupings and singing of the chorus contributed crucially to the overall impact of each show, ensuring that there was always an animated stage picture even when only one or two actors were in view. The practice of keeping the number of speaking actors normally restricted to three, with doubling of roles by the same actor where necessary, looks odd at first sight, but it makes sense in the special circumstance of Greek theatrical performance. Two factors are particularly relevant: first the use of masks, which was probably felt to be fundamental to shows associated with the cult of Dionysus and which made it easy for an actor to take more than one part within a single play, and second the need to concentrate the audience's attention by keeping the number of possible speakers limited. In a large, open acting area some kind of focusing device is important if the spectators are always to be sure where to direct their gaze. The Greek plays that have survived, particularly the tragedies, are extremely economical in their design, with no sub-plots or complications in the action which audiences might find distracting or confusing. Acting style, too, seems to have relied on large gestures and avoidance of fussy detail; we know from the size of some of the surviving theatres that many spectators would be sitting too far away to catch small-scale gestures or stage business. Some plays make powerful use of props, like Ajax's sword, Philoctetes' bow, or the head of Pentheus in *Bacchae*, but all these are carefully chosen to be easily seen and interpreted.

Above all, actors seem to have depended on their highly trained voices in order to captivate audiences and stir their emotions. By the middle of the fifth century there was a prize for the best actor in the tragic competition, as well as for the playwright and the financial sponsor of the performance (*chorēgos*), and comedy followed suit a little later. What was most admired in the leading actors who were entitled to compete for this prize was the ability to play a series of different and very demanding parts in a single day and to be a brilliant singer as well as a compelling speaker of verse: many of the main parts involve solo songs or complex exchanges between actor and chorus. Overall, the best plays and performances must have offered audiences a great charge of energy and excitement: the chance to see a group of chorusmen dancing and singing in a sequence of different guises, as young maidens, old counsellors, ecstatic maenads, and exuberant satyrs; to watch scenes in which supernatural beings – gods, Furies, ghosts – come into contact with human beings; to listen to intense debates and hear the blood-curdling offstage cries that heralded the arrival of a messenger with an account of terrifying deeds within, and then to see the bodies brought out and witness the lamentations. Far more 'happened' in most plays than we can easily imagine from the bare text on the page; this must help to account for the continuing appeal of drama throughout antiquity and across the Greco-Roman world.

From the fourth century onwards dramatic festivals became popular wherever there were communities of Greek speakers, and other gods besides Dionysus were honoured with performances of plays. Actors, dancers and musicians organised themselves for professional touring – some of them achieved star status and earned huge fees – and famous old plays were revived as part of the repertoire. Some of the plays that had been first performed for Athenian citizens in the fifth century became classics for very different audiences – women as well as men, Latin speakers as well as Greeks – and took on new kinds of meaning in their new environment. But theatre was very far from being an antiquarian institution: new plays, new dramatic forms like mime and pantomime, changes in theatre design, staging, masks and costumes all demonstrate its continuing vitality in the Hellenistic and Roman periods. Nearly all the Greek plays that have survived into modern times are ones that had a long theatrical life in antiquity; this perhaps helps to explain why modern actors, directors and audiences have been able to rediscover their power.

For further reading: entries in *Oxford Classical Dictionary* (3rd edition) under 'theatre staging, Greek' and 'tragedy, Greek'; J.R. Green, 'The theatre', Ch. 7 of *The Cambridge Ancient History, Plates to Volumes V and VI*, Cambridge, 1994; Richard Green and Eric Handley, *Images of the Greek Theatre*, London, 1995; Rush Rehm, *Greek Tragic Theatre*, London and New York, 1992; P.E. Easterling (ed.), *The Cambridge Companion to Greek Tragedy*, Cambridge, 1997; David Wiles, *Tragedy in Athens*, Cambridge, 1997.

Pat Easterling

Time line

Dates of selected authors and extant works

12th Century BC	**The Trojan war**	
8th Century BC	**HOMER**	• *The Iliad* • *The Odyssey*
5th Century BC 490–479 431–404	**The Persian wars** **The Peloponnesian wars**	

c. 525/4–456/5
 	
472
 	
456
	AESCHYLUS	(In probable order.)
		• *Persians*
		• *Seven against Thebes*
		• *Suppliants*
		• ***Oresteia Trilogy****:*
		  Agamemnon, Choephoroi
		  Eumenides
		• *Prometheus Bound*

c. 496/5–406 409 401 (posthumous)	**SOPHOCLES**	(Undated plays are in alphabetical order.) • *Ajax* • *Oedipus Tyrannus* • *Antigone* • *Trachiniae* • *Electra* • *Philoctetes* • *Oedipus at Colonus*
c. 490/80–407/6 438 (1st production 455) 431 428 415 412 409 ?408 ?408–6	**EURIPIDES**	(In probable order.) • *Alcestis* • *Medea* • *Heracleidae* • *Hippolytus* • *Andromache* • *Hecuba* • *Suppliant Women* • *Electra* • *Trojan Women* • *Heracles* • *Iphigenia among the Taurians* • *Helen* • *Ion* • *Phoenissae* • *Orestes* • *Cyclops* (satyr-play) • *Bacchae* • *Iphigenia at Aulis*
460/50–*c.* 386 411 405	**ARISTOPHANES**	(Selected works.) • *Thesmophoriazusae* • *Lysistrata* • *Frogs*
4th Century BC 384–322	**ARISTOTLE**	(Selected works.) • *The Art of Poetry*

Index

Bold numbers refer to pages. Other numbers are line references.

CPSIA information can be obtained
at www.ICGtesting.com
Printed in the USA
LVHW011752230820
663952LV00014B/974

9 780521 644808